Dragons

Dragons

Peter Hogarth with Val Clery

A
Jonathan-James
Book

A Studio Book
THE VIKING PRESS

A Jonathan-James Book

Published in 1979 by The Viking Press
625 Madison Avenue, New York, N.Y. 10022

Published simultaneously in Canada by
Penguin Books Canada Limited

Edited by R. Carolyn King
Jacket Painting and Alphabet by Kim La Fave
Picture Research by Elly Beintema
Printed in the United States of America by
R.R. Donnelley & Sons Company
Set in Trump Medieval

Jonathan-James Books
5 Sultan Street
Toronto, Ontario, Canada
M5S 1L6

Library of Congress Cataloging in Publication Data
Hogarth, Peter J.
   Dragons.
"A Jonathan-James book."
1. Dragons. I. Clery, Val, joint author. II. Title
GR830.D7H63   1980   398'.469   79-14699
ISBN 0-670-28176-X

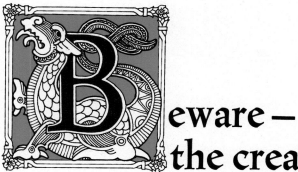eware —
the creatures
you may encounter
hereafter
have instilled
fear and wonder
in the minds and
hearts of men
since the dawn
of history...

Contents

The first dragon spawns a brood of ferocious monsters; from the depths they creep with horned heads, slithering coils, and forked tails, roaring, spewing fire – scaly creatures pitting supernatural powers against man in epic struggle.

Gods, heroes, and legendary dragon-slayers clash with the grisly creatures of the abyss, hurling down thunderbolts, destructive whirl-winds, and flashing lightning into their gaping jaws, to establish their supremacy in the universe over the crooked serpents of darkness.

88 MEDIEVAL

"Bestes, Peryllous and Terryble" still menace simple folk with deadly persistence, spreading clouds of poison and bloodcurdling fear into the darkest corners of the earth. But mankind is saved by heroes, saints, and martyrs and the loathsome creatures are dispatched in astonishing numbers.

164 RENAISSANCE

The printing press transmutes dragons into legend and fable, and phoenix-like they arise from the page in wondrous and uncharted lands, banished from civilization, yet still winding their steely coils around the minds of men the world over.

190 MODERN

As dragons sleep fitfully in the deepest corridors of men's imaginations, the scaly beasts begin to creep back from the fringes of the unknown world, and once again heroes and dragons confront each other in eternal combat to harness the powers of illusion and darkness.

A Classic Tale of Intrigue, Passion and Magic

The monster in his sheath of horny scales rolled forward his interminable coils, like the eddies of black smoke that spring from smoldering logs and chase each other from below in endless convolutions. But as he writhed he saw the maiden take her stand, and heard her in her sweet voice invoking Sleep, the conqueror of the gods, to charm him. She also called on the night-wandering Queen of the world below to countenance her efforts. Jason from behind looked on in terror. But the giant snake, enchanted by her song, was soon relaxing the whole length of his serrated spine and smoothing out his multitudinous undulations, like a dark and silent swell rolling across a sluggish sea. Yet his grim head still hovered over them, and the cruel jaws threatened to snap them up. But Medea, chanting a spell, dipped a fresh sprig of juniper in her brew and sprinkled his eyes with her most potent drug; and as the all-pervading magic scent spread around his head, sleep fell on him. Stirring no more, he let his jaw sink to the ground, and his innumerable coils lay stretched out far behind, spanning the deep wood. Medea called to Jason and he snatched the Golden Fleece from the oak. But she herself stayed where she was, smearing the wild one's head with a magic salve, till Jason urged her to come back to the ship and she left the somber grove of Ares.

The Voyage of the Argo

ANCIENT

A thousand years ago dragons were such familiar creatures that what they looked like and how they behaved was common knowledge to every man, woman, and child. No matter where they lived, everyone could describe dragons and dragon behavior in colorfully lurid detail. Dragons were as much a part of everyday life as the valiant heroes who vanquished the forces of evil to save mankind.

As recently as four hundred years ago, sightings of dragons seem to have been almost as frequent as sightings of whales today; and about that time dragons, too, were beginning to be an endangered species. But in the cen-turies prior to that in Europe, and more particularly in China where dragons had long played a leading role in mythology, factual accounts of their presence were commonplace. The evidence is not confined to works of natural history and literature but appears in everyday chronicles of events, in terms as prosaic as those referring to the state of the weather. And such eyewitness accounts are not derived from hearsay or anonymous rumor;

they were set down by people of some standing, by kings and knights, monks and archbishops, scholars and saints, whose word would scarcely be questioned. Reports of their presence may have suffered a severe decline meanwhile, but surely it is rather strange that they have never been erased from our imaginations? To understand their persistence it is necessary to look back to their origins, which coincide with the origins of human civilization.

Common beliefs took form when men began sharing life together. The earliest known communities of any size arose from the settlement of nomads on the fertile plains beside the rivers Tigris and Euphrates some time before 3000 B.C. Two distinct tribal groups inhabited this area, which coin-

OPPOSITE AND ABOVE *The epic eternal struggle between good and evil, order and chaos, darkness and light. The Babylonian god Marduk attacks his mother, Tiamat, the first dragon, with thunderbolts. Her defeat and death heralded the creation of Man, but not the end of dragons.*

The birth of the gods and the first dragon.

cides roughly with modern Iraq: in the north were the Sumerians, and in the south the Akkadians. About the year 1750 B.C. they were united under King Hammurabi into the empire of Babylon. Five hundred years later Babylon was invaded and conquered by another people from the north, the Assyrians. This intermingling of peoples, ideas, and traditions, enriched by trading contacts with other peoples in the rest of the known world, produced a flowering of culture. The stability of settled life depended on order, and on the communication and sharing of knowledge and belief. As a result the first writing, art, literature, science, and codified law developed in Babylonia during this period.

Communities, and the individuals who make them up, need an explanation of their existence and of the mysterious forces of the natural world around them. Probably for the first time, a complex and elaborate mythology and a coherent system of beliefs emerged from Babylonia. What we know of these beliefs is recorded on seven clay tablets in the form of a long poem known as the Babylonian Creation Epic. It is an account, similar in purpose to the first chapter of the Book of Genesis, of the creation of the universe, the birth of the gods, and how and why mankind came into existence.

In the beginning, according to the Creation Epic, there was neither land, nor gods, nor men; there were only two elements called Apsu and Tiamat. Apsu was male, the spirit of fresh water and the void in which the world existed; Tiamat was female and was the spirit of salt water and of primeval chaos. She is depicted as a monstrous being with a scaly serpentine body,

Another more vivid re-creation of the legendary end of Tiamat, with two of the dragon's other children supporting their brother Marduk in the attack. Similar family violence is common in the myths of Greek and Egyptian deities, as is the kinship of gods and monsters.

legs, and horns on her head. She was the first dragon, and her awesome ever-changing image has haunted mankind ever since. The fact that she was designated a female, fearsome and chaotic, may suggest that sexual discrimination also got off to an early start.

Eventually the union of Apsu and Tiamat, tempestuous and obscure at the best of times, was cursed rather than blessed with a large and oddly-assorted brood, amongst them the first gods of the primordial universe. The family, since myths are made by men, reflected on a vast scale the failings and stresses that tend to bedevil human family life. The new gods as they grew up obviously began to develop that unruly disrespect for parents that is still familiar, because the Epic records Apsu complaining bitterly to his wife, Tiamat, about their conduct:

> *Their ways are verily loathsome to me.*
> *By day I find no relief, nor repose at night.*
> *I will destroy, I will wreck their ways,*
> *That quiet may be restored. Let us have rest!*

Sentiments that parents through the ages might respond to, but Apsu meant what he said and could not be dissuaded by Tiamat's pleas for her children's lives. One of the young gods guessed what was intended, however, and struck first. Apsu himself was overpowered, tied up, and murdered.

Now Tiamat turned against her defiant offspring, determined to avenge her husband's death. To support her in this, she spawned another brood, a veritable army of ferocious monsters that included giant serpents, roaring dragons, lion-demons, the scorpion-man, and the centaur. The gods, meanwhile, well aware of their mother's vengeful plans, plotted their own strategy for the inevitable battle. They persuaded one of their number, Marduk, to face Tiamat in single combat. But he agreed only on condition that he would be made king of the entire universe if he were victorious. He armed himself with bow and arrow, club, fishing-net, a poisonous plant, and lightning, and he set out in a storm-chariot, escorted by the four winds.

Tiamat is slain and Marduk rules the universe.

Following a traditional exchange of threats and insults, the fight between mother and son began. And after an epic struggle, Tiamat was slain. Deprived of their leader, her supernatural army tried to flee, but Marduk snared them in his net and slew them also. From the body of one of Tiamat's supporters, Marduk took the Tablets of Destiny. With these, as supreme lord of the universe, he set about establishing a heaven and an earth, raised dry land above the waters, assigned appropriate functions to the various other gods, and appointed the moon as keeper of time. And finally, using the blood of one of the slain gods, he created "a savage — Man shall be his name — who shall be charged with serving the gods, so that they may be at ease."

To the people who inhabited Mesopotamia, the Creation Epic was much more than a common folktale. It was an explanation of the very existence of the universe and its workings; it described their own origin and defined their role in life. The solemn ritual recitation of the Epic on the fourth day of their New Year Festival was a highly important event; it ensured that all things would continue to function as ordained in the year ahead.

The conflict between Marduk and Tiamat is paralleled throughout history in legends of other lands. The dragon, while often attributed other names and other qualities, usually symbolizes evil or primeval chaos, which might explain a frequent association also with the sea and with storms — such unpredictable and violent forces of nature stir human dread even today. Similarly, the monstrous size attributed to Tiamat, indeed to most dragons, seems to confirm that human psychology has altered little through the centuries: we all tend to exaggerate what we find mysterious and threatening, yet seem to feel the need to visualize what we dread in some familiar form or other.

Images of dragons are very often vividly composed to suggest creatures that men normally fear — the coiling bodies of serpents, the wings and claws of bats or birds of prey, the savage jaws of crocodiles or lions, and the horns of other mammals, all exaggerated by word of mouth description or by the awe of religion.

Most of the forms in which Tiamat was originally depicted can be related to the ordinary creatures that people in the area had reason to hold in awe. The stealth and the speed of reptiles still awakens instinctive fear in humans, and the venomous snakes that exist to this day in the Middle East were probably more numerous in its primitive past. Dread may have been inflated further by nomads and traders circulating, with traditional exaggeration, tales of the

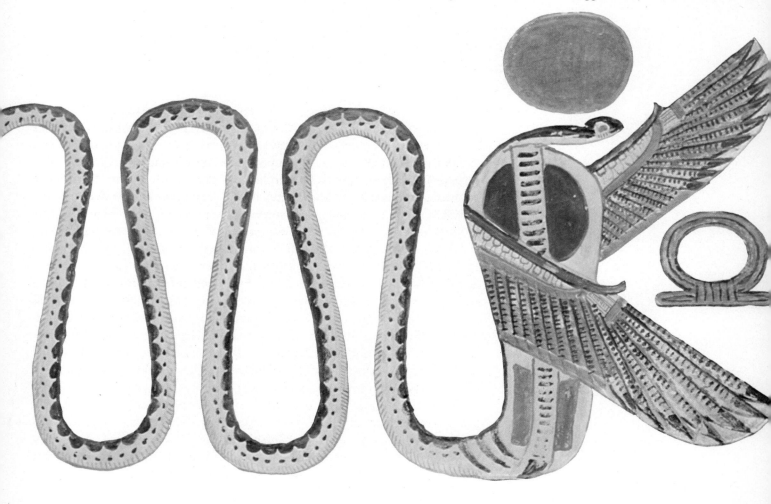

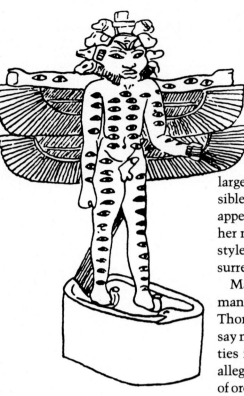

The deities of Egypt were depicted as strange amalgams of man and beast and monster, richly endowed with heads and eyes and arms. The myths of India and of Greece are haunted by creatures just as fantastic and incredible.

large snakes of India and even Africa. Imagination, once stimulated, is impossible to restrain. Horns were a very natural addition to Tiamat's threatening appearance; legs, drawn from the lizards also common to the region, added to her mobility, as did the claws and wings of a bat or a bird of prey. The artistic style admired in the depiction of dragons has never been realism, but rather surrealism.

Marduk, too, although strictly a Babylonian deity, has populated legend in many guises throughout history; he is the original ancestor of gods such as Thor, heroes such as Sir Lancelot, and saints, with St. George the favorite, to say nothing of countless local champions who have delivered their communities from the threat of dragons. The hero who overcomes the dragon is an allegory that still portrays what most of us wish: the triumph of good over evil, of order over chaos and, less certainly nowadays, of man over nature. Marduk's acquisition of the Tablets of Destiny seems to underline that wishful moral incentive that virtue will be rewarded. This theme recurs in many later legends, with the tablets often replaced by rewards of great riches, either spiritual or material: the secret of the first form of writing, the ability to understand the language of animals or to foresee the future, or sometimes the discovery of gold or precious stones.

In our time we may feel ourselves beyond the need for such childish allegories, but they have served every society throughout human history in coming to terms with the puzzle of existence. They reduce what is vast and incomprehensible to a scale that man can grasp. Like the creatures that inhabit them, allegories themselves defy time and space and assume many disguises. We should not be too certain that what we assume to be commonsense explanations today will not prove to have been allegories tomorrow.

Surviving fragments of trade goods and household objects have enabled archaeologists to trace the often immense journeys made by traders throughout the ancient world. Many ideas of the ancient world may never have been recorded, and only fragments of those that were recorded have survived, so it is difficult to trace the spread of ideas. But given the notorious loquacity of today's salesmen, it is not unreasonable to suppose that the traders of the ancient world exchanged prevailing myths and legends as well as durable goods. It should not be surprising then that the vivid theme of a god slaying a monstrous serpent or dragon recurs in the creation myths of the Assyrians, who shared Mesopotamia with the Babylonians, or indeed in the myths of three neighboring peoples of the ancient Near East: the Egyptians, the Hittites, and the Canaanites. In a world so full of uncertainties, legends that seemed to provide some answers and certainly a few thrills and chills, were probably amongst the most salable commodities.

To the Egyptians, monstrous serpents or dragons seem to have symbolized many different things. A written scroll of the New Kingdom, which dates after 1580 B.C., briefly mentions the victory of the god Seth over a serpentine monster representing the sea. While the conflict bears some resemblance to that of Marduk and Tiamat, it seems less important. Seth, brother of Isis and Osiris and son of Earth and Sky, is a god of strange and contradictory personality and of bizarre appearance: he is shown either as an animal with a long drooping snout, square ears, and a forked tail, or as a human figure with a similar head – a head that might have been modeled on that of an elephant. Elephants and dragons were to develop an odd relationship in later legends.

Another creature of Egyptian mythology is the divine serpent Sito, reputed to encircle the world with its immense coils and also represented in several

The gods and goddesses of Egyptian mythology had a confusing tendency to change form, sometimes depicted in human guise, sometimes part human and part animal, and sometimes as serpent-dragons or as symbols of the natural phenomena they represented.

other mythologies. Sito is often merely depicted in the form of a circle, holding its tail in its mouth.

A somewhat more meaningful and coherent Egyptian legend concerns the daily defeat of the serpent-dragon Apep, which is told in this way: Every morning the sun god Ra, Lord of the Sky, embarks in his boat and sets sail from east to west across the celestial waters (in earthly terms, the River Nile). Ra is perpetually threatened by Apep, who attempts time after time to engulf the frail boat of the sun in darkness. Occasionally during the daylight hours, at the time of a solar eclipse for example, Apep does gain a brief ascendancy. But otherwise, the greatest threat to Ra occurs each night as the god passes through the realm of darkness. Apep attempts to overthrow Ra and destroy the sun, but each night he is repulsed by Ra's supporters so that the sun may rise again. The chief defender of Ra is the enigmatic god Seth, who rides in the bow of the boat.

Seth plays a dramatic and more significant role in an account of the struggle given in the thirty-ninth chapter of the Book of the Dead, a hieroglyphic text that has partially survived from a period between 1590 and 1320 B.C. The graphic account of the defeat of Apep includes stage directions, suggesting that the text may have been a script for a ritual performance of the legend.

At the beginning of the surviving portion of text, Seth orders Apep to retreat: "Back, villain! Plunge into the depths of the Abyss! If you speak, your face will be overturned by the gods. Your heart will be seized by the lynx, your reins will be bound by the scorpion."

Seth's bluster seems to work. After some further abuse (and possibly with the aid of the other gods in Ra's celestial crew) Apep is forced to surrender

Every day the dragon Apep attempts to halt the voyage of the sun god Ra across the celestial waters and to plunge the world into darkness. And every day the god Seth, as fearsome in appearance as the dragon, drives the monster off.

Egyptian winged creatures combined the symbolic menace of a world serpent with its interminable coils, and the powerful wings of a bird of prey.

and is tied up. Seth reports that Apep has been defeated and that "the spirits of the reddening sky have trapped him." Ra continues safely on his voyage and dawn breaks.

Apep, it turns out, is not completely cowed. He begins to taunt Seth, reminding him that during a previous encounter with his own nephew, he was castrated. Stung by this gibe, Seth tricks Apep into looking the other way, decapitates him, and cuts his body into pieces. Each night the violent sequence is the same: threats, the capture of Apep, his taunts, and his eventual death at the hands of an enraged Seth.

After the death of Apep, the drama takes a curious turn. The boastful Seth speaks disparagingly of the sun god's possessions (including the sun itself, and other sacred objects), and patronizingly announces that since he has slain Apep, the other gods are sufficient to look after Ra. He threatens to overturn Ra's boat with storms if he is not accorded proper respect, but for this arrogance Seth is dismissed from the boat.

Seth's history is ambiguous. He slays Apep in defence of Ra, which seems to align him with the forces of light, life, and virtue. However, he is also responsible for the grisly slaying and dismemberment of his older brother, the god Osiris. As god of storms, Seth is associated with other chaotic natural forces: thunder, earthquakes, the hot winds from the desert, drought, confusion, illness, and death. Ultimately Seth comes to be regarded not as a force of good, but as the incarnation of evil.

Seth has been identified with Typhon, a creature of Greek mythology manifested as a monster with one hundred dragons' heads. Eventually Typhon was slain by a thunderbolt hurled by Zeus. So Seth, a hero who slays a dragon on behalf of the gods, is not rewarded by great riches, but is himself transformed into a monster and is slain by a god. He is not the last dragonslayer to suffer an unexpected and ironic fate.

Anatolia in eastern Turkey was the homeland of the Hittites. It is a country of mountains and valleys where storms and clouds are frequent. This may account for the great importance in Hittite religion of the storm or

21

weather god, referred to as "King of Heaven, Lord of the Land of Hatti." In Hittite legends of The Slaying of the Dragon, it is this weather god who plays the heroic role. It will be recalled that Marduk, too, was a god of storms, who used lightning as his weapon.

Two versions of the Hittite dragon myth remain. In the earlier of the two, the story reveals that the weather god has suffered defeat in a previous encounter with the dragon Illuyankas. He appeals to the other gods for help, and the goddess Inaras volunteers a plan. She prepares a sumptuous banquet with barrels of every kind of drink. Then she calls upon a mortal, Hupasiyas, to assist her. He agrees to, if she will make love with him. Having done so, Inaras calls the dragon to come out of his lair and enjoy the banquet.

At the world's end, according to St. John the Divine, an angel with a key will lay hold on the dragon, which is Satan, and will cast him down and lock him in a bottomless pit "till a thousand years be fulfilled."

So up came the Dragon with his children; they ate and drank and emptied every barrel and quenched their thirst. They were not able to go back into their hole. So Hupasiyas came up and bound the Dragon with a rope. Then the weather god came and slew the Dragon Illuyankas, and the gods were with him.

The legend has a cryptic sequel. As further reward, Inaras built the mortal Hupasiyas a house on a cliff in the land of Tarukka. But she ordered him never to look out of the window on any account, lest he should see his wife and children. After twenty days in the house, Hupasiyas could no longer

ABOVE *The fearful feathered creature
decorating an ancient Aztec shield
might easily be mistaken for the griffin
or Chimera of Mediterranean myth.*

RIGHT *Tlazolteotl, Aztec goddess
of witchcraft, rides on a serpent, the
symbol of sexuality. Her broom, unlike
the brooms of European witches, is
intended to sweep away the sins of
mankind.*

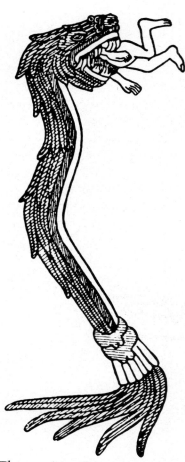

The voracious man-eating serpent-dragon of Aztec legend may well have derived from tales of the South American anaconda and the boa-constrictor, the largest snakes in existence.

ABOVE AND BELOW *The origin of the Aztec people remains a mystery. But aspects of their legendary art, and their belief in dragons, suggest links either with Egypt or with Asia.*

resist the temptation. He pushed the window open and did see his wife and children. It is difficult to follow what happened next because the tablet recording the legend becomes fragmentary and unintelligible, but there seems to have been a quarrel, with Hupasiyas being killed by the goddess.

In a later version the dragon seems to have gained possession of the eyes and heart of the weather god during a fight at the banquet. As a means of recovering these organs and avenging himself, he conceives a son by a mortal woman. When the son is of age, he marries the daughter of the dragon Illuyankas and persuades his new father-in-law to give him the weather god's heart and eyes as a gift. He restores these to his father, who immediately resumes combat with the dragon and slays him. He also slays his own son, at the son's request.

Religious significance seems lacking in these fragmentary versions of the Hittite dragon-slaying myths. The mythic scale of the battle between Tiamat and Marduk is absent and the elements of trickery and jealousy have a human pettiness about them more suited to a folktale than to a creation myth. Nevertheless, some form of the legend of The Slaying of the Dragon did have as important a place in the Hittite religion as in the Babylonian and apparently was recited or reenacted solemnly in the course of a major religious ceremony.

OPPOSITE AND ABOVE *Judeo-Christian art through the ages reflects the prevalence of dragons, the ever-threatening agents of chaos and evil, against which only faith, prayer, and divine intervention might prevail.*

Not far to the south of the Hittite homeland lay the land of the Canaanites. Much of their mythology centers on the epic of a god with the title of Baal, meaning "The Lord." (Marduk, god of the Babylonians, was known additionally by the similar title of Bel.) Baal's proper name is given as Haddad, meaning "Thunderer." According to one passage of the epic, he

... will send abundance of his rain
And he will utter his voice in the clouds,
He will send his flashing to the earth with lightning.

Here again is a god of storms like Marduk, like the weather god of the Hittites, and in some ways like the Egyptian god Seth. Unlike the destruc-

tive Seth, however, Baal appears to be a fertility god, whose benign rainfall fosters the growth of vegetation and food crops. A common preoccupation with the power of weather among the peoples of the ancient world is understandable, but the similarity of names and titles in gods of different religions seems to confirm that, despite the rudimentary means of travel and communication, ideas were as widely traded as goods.

Two episodes in the legendary life of Baal are of particular relevance. The first is a description of how he asserts his divine authority over the threatening ocean, establishing order over chaos. Incited by a fellow god, Baal takes a magical mace and proceeds, after striking the god Sea "between the eyes" to "drive Sea from his throne, even Ocean Current from the seat of his sovereignty." While Ocean is not here incarnated as a monstrous dragon, the myth does bear a symbolic resemblance to its earlier Babylonian counterpart. Since Canaan was situated along what is now the coast of Israel, its people would have had personal experience of the vast and unpredictable power of the sea.

In the second instance, Baal fought and slew a monster so obviously dragon-like as to recall the Mesopotamian Tiamat:

... thou didst smite Lotan the Primeval Serpent,
And didst annihilate the Crooked Serpent,
The Close-coiling One of Seven Heads ...

Many-headed dragons, particularly those with seven heads, abound in mythology. An Akkadian seal of about 2200 B.C. shows one being attacked by two gods and their supporters. And in the myths of classical Greece and Rome, the hero Hercules kills the seven-headed Hydra of the Lernean Swamp; indeed the Hydra persists in legend through the Middle Ages and beyond. It is difficult to discover exactly why myth assigns so many monsters seven heads but the number, rich in symbolic meanings, is linked

OPPOSITE AND ABOVE *It accorded conveniently with medieval theology that a dragon might be the Devil in disguise, or at least a manifestation of satanic power.*

RIGHT *Dragons sometimes got embroiled in theological disputes. Originally, the apocalyptic beast in this illustration from Luther's translation of the New Testament wore the papal crown. But in later editions the insulting detail was amended.*

to the essential orders of the cosmos and the Seven Directions of Space. As will be seen, the legend of Baal slaying the dragon Lotan undergoes many permutations throughout ancient literature and throughout history.

What is now known as the Old Testament came into being around A.D. 100. Jewish religious leaders met to decide which of the scriptures were to be accepted as canonical — that is, constituting the official doctrine of their religion. A number of texts were excluded, and these are known as the apocryphal books of the Old Testament.

The first chapters of the Book of Genesis contain the Hebrew account of the creation of the world. But there are two separate and conflicting accounts of creation. In the older account, the primeval universe is seen as waterless, the process of creation beginning when "there went up a mist from the earth, and watered the whole face of the ground." The alternative myth with which the Book of Genesis opens is thought to have been written after the Jewish exile in Babylon. And it shows clear similarities to the Babylonian Creation Epic, describing the original state of the universe not as an arid waste, but as watery chaos. God divided the waters, created land, vegetation, animals, man and woman; in some particulars the process repeats Marduk's creative activities.

In several other respects, too, the biblical account shows the influence of prevailing mythologies in the Near East. Here is one instance:

Thou didst divide the sea by thy strength:
Thou breakest the heads of the dragons in the waters.
Thou breakest the heads of Leviathan in pieces,
And gavest him to be meat to the people inhabiting the wilderness.

The god slaying the dragon motif appears once more, closely resembling the Canaanite legend of Baal ("The Lord") slaying Lotan: the dragon's name is vaguely similar; it has many heads (although the number is not specified); and the meaning of the god's title, Jehovah, is identical in translation.

Leviathan surfaces sporadically throughout the Old Testament in varying symbolic guises. Sometimes he is not an evil monster of the deep, but merely a denizen of the "great and wide sea" and of no special significance. By far the most detailed description occurs in the Book of Job. The fact that

OPPOSITE AND RIGHT *Just as the Greeks depended on their gods and heroes to deliver them from the threat of dragons, so Christians put their trust in saints and archangels to rid them of the monsters.*

the monster here has but a single head, and seems to be armored with scales so close that no weapon can penetrate, might be attributable to the Jews' captivity in Egypt where they must have seen crocodiles in the Nile. But the burning gaze and fire-breathing mouth ascribed to Leviathan in Job were to become traditional characteristics of the dragon for many centuries to come. Which is not to imply that seven-headed dragons became extinct; they, too, persisted in classical and medieval legend.

Subsequently Hebrew legend was to embroider considerably on the biblical Leviathan. Like the Egyptian Sito, or the later Nordic Serpent of Midgard, he also held his tail between his teeth and girdled the globe with his coils. He

Given that dragons were evil, it took only a little stretch of the imagination to believe that a seductive dragon, rather than a mere serpent, had brought about Man's fall from Paradise.

had as many eyes as days of the week, again seven, and scales that outshone the sun. He could engulf the waters of the River Jordan and was reputed to feed on other mighty dragons. A Hebrew chronicler claimed that while he was crossing the great sea, he saw a beast raise its head above the waves, and on its two horns was engraved the message: "This tiny sea-creature, measuring hardly three hundred leagues, is on his way to serve as Leviathan's food." Surely this must stand as a very early example of the promotional hyperbole we may have imagined a part only of modern life.

Sometimes Leviathan changes gender and contends with her deadliest enemy, Behemoth, who has a tail like a cedar tree, bones as strong as iron or

Leviathan, the vast fire-breathing dragon of the deep, whose flesh will feed the righteous on the Day of Judgment, and whose skin will clothe the walls of Jerusalem in brilliance.

Dragons continue to multiply despite holy intervention.

brass, and an even more formidable thirst, being able to consume a year's flow of Jordan water in a single gulp. Leviathan and Behemoth, created together, are destined to slay each other on the Day of Judgment. On that day the flesh of Leviathan is to be given as food to the righteous, part of its skin will serve as a tent for them, and the remainder is to cover the walls of Jerusalem. Its brilliant scales will make the city visible to the ends of the earth.

Amongst the Apocrypha is the Book of Bel and the Dragon, formerly part of the Book of Daniel. It relates how Daniel, during the Jews' captivity in Babylon, became the friend and adviser of King Cyrus. The principal local deity was Bel, worshiped in the form of an immense brass idol. Worshipers were obliged to deliver for the god's consumption each day twelve measures of fine flour, forty sheep, and six barrels of wine. Suspicious of the idol's vast appetite Daniel, by means of a cunning ruse, managed to demonstrate to Cyrus that in fact the priests of Bel and their families had been growing fat on the sacrificial offerings.

In the same temple the Babylonians were also required to worship a huge

The insatiable beasts of the Apocalypse, Leviathan the dragon and its eternal enemy the satanic Behemoth,
needed to be placated continually by
sacrifice.

dragon. Even Daniel was convinced that it was not simply a brass idol. But he disposed of it just as summarily by means of another ruse. Making up a concoction of pitch, fat, and other flammable materials, he fed this to the dragon, which immediately burst fierily asunder and died on the spot.

Daniel's original method of slaying a dragon was to become accepted practice. According to folklore it was used, for example, by King Cracus of the town of Krakow in eastern Poland and by the heroes of at least three encounters with dragons in Scotland alone. Since the fiery-mouthed dragons themselves ignited the materials ingested, the method had much to commend it.

Finally — and the word was never more appropriate — dragons play as important a role in the end of the world as they did in its beginning. Both the Old Testament and the Apocrypha contain scattered allusions to Jewish beliefs concerning the Day of Judgment when, for example, "the Lord with his sore and great and strong sword shall punish Leviathan the piercing serpent, even Leviathan that crooked serpent; he shall slay that dragon that is in the sea."

By far the most vivid of the myths foretelling the end of it all are offered by St. John the Divine in the Book of Revelations. Although at times the narrative seems about to sink under the weight of its symbolism, the overall effect is of a maelstrom of highly colored and often terrifying images building

The Old Testament prophets were tormented by horrendous visions. A Renaissance print depicts Daniel's nightmare of the allegorical monsters that were to fall upon the tribes of Israel and rend them apart.

RIGHT *No work of literature so inflamed the imaginations of medieval artists as the apocalyptic Revelations of St. John the Divine. The projection of ferocious dragons into everyday settings of the time was truly terrifying.*

OPPOSITE *St. John envisioned a cataclysmic assault on mankind by dragons and monsters of every description. Since sinners were to be the prime victims, such pictures had a powerful effect on contemporary morality.*

RIGHT *Not content with the effect of dragons, artists heightened the terror by reflecting the recurrent warfare that bedeviled Europe in the Middle Ages. And according to St. John, war between the nations was to herald the approach of the Apocalypse and the onslaught of the beasts.*

RIGHT   *The idea that dragons may have derived their form from primeval dinosaurs is historically fallacious, but it is not impossible that they were inspired partly by the crocodiles of the Nile delta.*

While the biblical account of Daniel's encounter with a dragon in Babylon was not included in the authorized Old Testament, it persisted in religious art throughout the Middle Ages. Dragons were sometimes reduced to the incongruous scale of very ordinary wild beasts.

The Prophet & the Dragon

And in that same place there was a great dragon, which they of Babylon worshiped. And the king said unto Daniel, "Wilt thou say that this is of brass? Lo, he liveth, and eateth and drinketh; thou canst not say that he is no living god: therefore worship him." Then said Daniel, "I will worship the Lord my God: for He is a living God.

But give me these, O king, and I shall slay this dragon without sword or staff." The king said, "I give thee these." Then Daniel took pitch, and fat, and hair, and did seethe them together, and made lumps thereof: this he put in the dragon's mouth, so the dragon did eat and burst in sunder: and Daniel said "Lo! These are

the gods ye worship."
    When they of Babylon heard that, they took great indignation, and conspired against the king saying, "The king is become a Jew, and he hath pulled down Bel, and slain the dragon."
Apocryphal Book of Bel and the Dragon

A fourteenth-century panel in the Church of St. Etienne in Mulhouse shows Daniel about to dose the dragon with his fatal inflammatory pill. His ingenuity was to be repeated by several later dragon-slayers.

relentlessly to a climax, followed by a more tranquil vision of a "new heaven and a new earth."

First there appears a red dragon having "seven heads and ten horns, and seven crowns upon his heads." Michael and his angels fight the dragon and cast him out of heaven onto the earth. Then, in the words of St. John, the Beast of the Apocalypse appears:

> *And I stood upon the sand of the sea, and saw a beast rise up out of the sea, having seven heads and ten horns, and upon his horns ten crowns, and upon his heads the name of blasphemy. And the beast which I saw was like unto a leopard, and his feet were as the feet of a bear, and his mouth was the mouth of a lion: and the dragon gave him his power, and his seat, and great authority.*
> *... And I saw an angel come down from heaven, having the key of the bottomless pit and a great chain in his hand. And he laid hold on the dragon, that old serpent, which is the Devil, and Satan, and bound him a thousand years, and cast him into the bottomless pit, and shut him up, and set a seal on him, that he should deceive the nations no more, till a thousand years should be fulfilled.*

Since this was prophecy, and since the Day of Judgment has yet to arrive, dragons have yet to have *that* fate visited upon them.

India, like every civilization with a developed mythology, has numerous legends of dragons or of monstrous and supernatural serpents. Set midway between the ancient cultures of West and East, with obvious trading links in

RIGHT AND BELOW *The heroes of
ancient Persia, like their counterparts
in classical Greece, were often required
to prove their valor by confronting and
slaying dragons. An interchange of
legends between the adjacent cultures
seems probable, just as the artistic style
suggests the influence of nearby India.*

OPPOSITE *Contrary to the peaceful
impression of this ancient Persian
scene, tradition held that dragons and
elephants maintained an age-old
enmity toward each other.*

BELOW *Vishnu, the most revered of India's gods, reclines on the giant serpent Ananta, The Endless One, guarded by the reptile's eleven cobra-like heads. Ananta is considered the symbol of cosmic energy, playing a vital role in the process of creation.*

OPPOSITE *Krishna dancing on Kaliya's back. According to Hindu tradition, there is no conflict between god and serpent, both being manifestations of the same divine nature.*

both directions, its dragon myths have been exposed to influence on the one hand from those of the Near East and, on the other, from the flourishing traditions of the Chinese dragon.

Indian myths, in common with those of the West, seek to explain the nature and origin of the universe. Familiarly, out of the cosmic waters of the Abyss were created the earth, the upper, and the infernal regions. Dominant in all this is an enormous serpent known as Ananta, protected by the monster's nine heads, their hoods expanded. The hoods suggest that the idea of Ananta may have derived from the indigenous cobra, but orthodox belief maintains the opposite, that Ananta is the progenitor (and ruler) of all ordinary serpents. Unlike Tiamat and many other serpentine monsters, includ-

ing some also inhabiting Indian legend, Ananta is never slain. He remains unscathed because his is an alternative manifestation of the divine nature of Vishnu: in this instance, god-hero and monster are one and the same.

In the beginning the processes of creation were under constant attack from the antagonistic forces of chaos, and every so often the ordered universe

The god Vishnu floats across the waters of the cosmos on the back of the serpent-dragon Ananta.

would be reduced to its primeval state. The force of chaos was personified as another monster, a giant serpent of the Abyss, whose threats had to be repulsed by the direct intervention of Vishnu.

In the course of one such assault, the serpent of chaos succeeded, seizing the freshly-formed Earth and carrying her off into the lowest depths of the cosmic sea. Vishnu immediately assumed the form of a giant boar. While the boar is a warm-blooded animal of the earthly sphere, its habitual reveling in swamps makes it familiar with the watery element. So in this very appropriate form Vishnu plunged into the cosmic sea, vanquished the giant serpent, and rescued Earth.

Another Indian myth in the tradition of dragon slaying involves a clash between the demonic dragon Vritra and the god Indra. Vritra, the "Enveloper" or "Obstructor," is depicted as a limbless cloud serpent, writhing about the mountain tops and holding the waters of heaven in its belly. Indra is a weather god who rides the skies in a chariot and is armed with the rainbow and the lightning. He launches a thunderbolt at Vritra; the dragon bursts asunder and the pent-up waters stream down freely across the thirsty land, bringing new life to all.

The pertinence of such a legend in a parched land like India is obvious. Rain is crucial to survival; it does indeed come from the formation and bursting of clouds in the mountains, accompanied by thunder. Even if the sequence is more fanciful than scientific, the identification of cloud as a water-retaining dragon and thunderbolts as weapons of a heroic god is vividly effective as a religious myth.

Again, this myth shows a close resemblance to other dragon-slaying myths. Indra is a weather god, like the Hittite Baal and the Nordic Thor. The dragon, like so many others, plays a vital role in the supply of life-sustaining water; indeed dragon-serpents, because of their undulating motion, are widely regarded as the traditional symbol of water. In some versions of this Indian myth, Indra is slain and is resurrected, or is swallowed and later regurgitated by Vritra. This, as will be seen, becomes a common feature of dragon-slaying myths.

Indian mythology encompasses also a host of lesser supernatural snake-like beings, the nagas. Being semi-divine, they had the ability to change shape and are often depicted partially or wholly in human form. But they also assumed the appearance of giant snakes or creatures resembling the conventional dragon. One model, for example, is described as having wings, the upper part of the body in human form but with a horned ox-head, and the lower body coiling and serpentine like a dragon. Female nagas, when resembling a human shape, were renowned for their beauty, cleverness, and charm. Minor princely families of India were inclined to boast of numbering a *nagini* among their ancestors.

In addition to diversity of form, the nagas seem to have served in a remarkable variety of roles both in the heaven and on the earth of ancient India. A contemporary Chinese commentator lists the four main classes into which nagas were divided. First there were the celestial nagas who guarded and held aloft the Heavenly Palace. Then followed the divine nagas who made clouds rise and rain fall. Next, the earthly nagas ensured that streams and rivers flowed freely. And finally, there existed a class of nagas who lived in hiding, guarding treasure, and bestowing blessings on mankind.

Nagas are to be found in the ancient carvings that adorn the doors of both Hindu and Buddhist temples, posed in attitudes of pious devotion. This suggests a connection between Eastern and Western mythology, because in the works of classical authors such as Pliny and in the medieval writings that derive from them, it is mentioned that a carved dragon's head at the threshold of a house will protect it from evil influences. Mere coincidence seems less likely as an explanation than the migration of the tradition by means of traders from one culture to the other.

Nagas are endowed with magic powers.

Nagas were reputed to carry precious pearls in their foreheads and to have considerable magic powers. Those powers were not always used beneficially: when annoyed, nagas were capable of killing people with their breath — a dragon-like ability — and of causing drought, pestilence, and great suffering. They might be forgiven some petulance; apparently they had much to put up with. According to an account written in the third century A.D.:

A golden-winged Garuda bird, one of the many torments endured by nagas, the usually benign dragons of Indian mythology.

The naga has to endure three kinds of suffering: his delicious food turns into toads as soon as he takes it into his mouth; his beautiful women, as well as he himself, change into serpents when he tries to embrace them; on his back he has scales lying in a reverse direction [pointing forwards] and when sand and pebbles enter between them, he suffers pains that pierce his heart. Therefore do not envy him.

If those torments were not proof enough against human envy, a Chinese authority heaps further distress on the sorry lot of the nagas: hot winds and hot sand that burn their skin, flesh, and bones; sudden violent tornados that blow away their palaces, along with their treasures and their clothes, leaving them without the means to disguise themselves as humans; and golden-winged Garuda birds which enter their palaces and devour their children.

The fact that nagas lived in palaces may have provided some consolation for their other miseries. Western dragons had to be content, for the most part, with nothing grander than holes or "... depe caves of the grounde." The nagas — notably the eight great Naga Kings — did live with their retinues in the most splendid jeweled and golden palaces. These lay under the earth or, more usually, at the bottom of lakes or rivers. (The Dragon Kings of China were similarly housed.) Humans occasionally enjoyed hospitality in these establishments, some for lengthy periods. Presumably it is to these we owe the vivid descriptions of their magnificence.

Buddha is seated on the coils and sheltered by the hooded heads of the naga king Mucilinda.

Such munificence underlines the fact that nagas seldom shared the animosity towards men that is common to most other dragons; indeed, they seem to have been lavish in the benefits they bestowed. One man was taught by a naga king to understand the language of animals. And one of the greatest of Buddhist philosophers, Nagarjuna ("Arjuna of the nagas"), owed at least some of his reputation to the wisdom imparted to him by the nagas. This included the belief that all is void, that the soul neither exists nor does not exist ... that it is neither eternal nor finite. It may be that this philosophical stance had some bearing on the nonchalant termination of Nagarjuna's career – in either 212 B.C. or A.D. 194, he cut off his own head as a religious offering.

One naga king had an encounter with the Buddha himself. In the fifth week after attaining Perfect Enlightenment, the Buddha came to the shore of Lake Mucilinda. There he remained, motionless and rapt in contemplation at the foot of a great tree. The rain began to fall and continued without a break on all four continents. The naga king Mucilinda, guardian of the lake, rose to the surface of the water, and saw the darkness of the rain clouds. To protect the Buddha from the elements, Mucilinda wrapped him round seven times with his coils, and spread his seven hoods as an umbrella. After seven days, the rain stopped and Mucilinda, assuming the shape of a youth, paid homage to the Great Being.

It is possible that the Buddha's links with nagas may have been even closer. He was said, in some accounts of his early life, to have been born as the naga king Bhuridatta in a jeweled pavilion beneath the sacred River Jumna, or as one of a number of other naga kings in similar sacred rivers or lakes.

As well as being the patron spirits of lakes and rivers, nagas were of course the controllers of rainfall. Clouds and thunder were considered manifestations of a naga's wrath. From a single drop of water one naga could deluge three kingdoms with rain, or prevent the sea from drying up. There were many incantations and complex rituals for inducing a naga to produce rain; often they involved painting pictures of a number of nagas with cow-dung on the walls of temples over three periods of seven days.

As rainmakers, nagas shared a curious affinity with elephants. According to legend elephants, in days long ago, had wings and roamed freely around the sky, consorting with clouds. This stirs up, irrepressibly if inappropriately, images of the animated film *Dumbo* by the late Walt Disney. Unhappily,

The Tree & the Naga King

The asoka tree is a strange one: It will not flower unless it is touched and kicked by a girl or young woman. Odder still is the story of a particular asoka tree. This stood, alone, in the forest of Vindhya. Beneath it was a lake, and in this lake the splendid palace of the mighty Naga King Paravataksha. Paravataksha had in his possession a peerless sword, obtained from the war of the gods and the demons. A certain ascetic coveted this sword. To obtain it, he approached the tree and scattered enchanted mustard-seed on the water of the lake, so clearing it of the dust which obscured it. He then began to utter magical incantations suitable for vanquishing serpents. These were soon effective, and defeated the earthquakes and stormclouds brought forth by the monster. Then from the asoka tree emerged a heavenly nymph, murmuring spells, with her jeweled ornaments gently tinkling. Approaching the ascetic, she pierced his soul with a sidelong glance of love. At this, he lost his self-control. As the apparition embraced him, he forgot all of his serpent-defeating incantations. At this, the ferocious Naga King came out of his palace, his eyes like flames, roaring horribly. But the ascetic had died of a broken heart.

Myths and Symbols in Indian Art

Elephants are cursed and brought down to earth.

however, a flight of elephants at one time chanced to alight on the branch of a tree overhanging the spot where a great sage was instructing his pupils. Not unnaturally, the branch broke and deposited elephants on the pupils below, killing several. The irate sage laid a curse on the elephants, depriving them both of their wings and of their divine ability to transform themselves into clouds. Nevertheless, earthbound though they may be, elephants are said to retain their affinity with clouds and to be capable, like nagas, of bestowing the blessing of rainfall on mankind. A sacred elephant is known by the same word as the serpent divinity; it, too, is called a naga. This Oriental link is particularly interesting because in the West, also, there persists the myth of an incongruous and less happy relationship between elephants and dragons. There, by tradition, the dragon lies in wait for the elephant, entwines it in its scaly coils, and kills it. In terms of physical appearance an elephant's trunk does resemble a serpent, its ears look like rudimentary wings, and its gray body is as amorphous as a cloud.

It will be recalled that in Egypt, which surely must have had some contact with India, the ambiguous weather god Seth, sometimes aligned with divine order and sometimes with chaos, was traditionally depicted with an elephantine head. While mostly benign in their influence, nagas share many similarities with the maligned dragons of the West: both possessed supernatural powers; both inhabited rivers and lakes, and controlled the availability of water; and both were guardians of great riches, spiritual and material. As will be seen, the many dragons of China do not differ greatly from those of India and the West.

Elephants, in Indian legend, have an affinity with clouds and share with nagas the power to provide rain. Due to an unfortunate incident they were deprived of an ability to fly by a Buddhist sage.

The Limits of Art

About the sixth century, the painter Chang Seng-yu was in the process of executing a wall painting that depicted four dragons. Passers-by criticized his work, complaining quite correctly that he had left out the eyes of the dragons. Eventually the angry artist could tolerate the criticism no longer. In a rage, he picked up his brushes and painted in the eyes of two of the figures. Immediately the air was filled with thunder and lightning, the wall split asunder, and the two completed dragons ascended to heaven. Only the eyeless dragons remained.

According to tradition, China's history dates back to 3000 B.C. Modern historians tend, however, to set its beginnings in the Shang dynasty, about 1600 B.C., and to dismiss accounts of earlier rulers and events as mythical. Given that this is a study of dragons, the dispute must seem somewhat academic. But whichever view is right, Chinese history remains undeniably ancient and remarkably coherent. And its culture, despite continual invasions, civil wars, and natural catastrophes has proved more stable and enduring than most other cultures.

The Chinese dragon has shared this stability and endurance. A clay vessel dating from about 2000 B.C. bears the representation of a dragon-like creature – a wingless reptile with a large head, a long body, and two clawed feet; like dragons encountered elsewhere, owing something to the crocodile and something to the serpent. While there may have been a native tradition of dragons far pre-dating this piece of evidence, dragons in China inevitably showed the stamp of foreign design.

The most obvious imported influence, along with Buddhism, came from India. As the religion took root and flourished in the spiritual soil of China, so the naga, a creature of Buddhist tradition, supplanted or transformed similar creatures of Chinese myth. The Chinese *Lung wang*, or Dragon Kings, closely resemble the Indian Naga Kings. They, too, were patron divinities of rivers, lakes, and the sea; suitably propitiated, they could deliver rain; unsuitably offended, they could withold it, or even cause storms and floods. Like nagas, they were reputed to carry a pearl of great worth, but in their throats rather than their foreheads. They too lived in magnificent underwater palaces. According to a sailors' legend current in 900 B.C., one such palace was located under a small island that lay five or six days' sailing from Su-cheu, in

A Chinese dragon emblem worn by a mandarin of the Imperial civil service. Yellow dragons were considered superior to those of other colors, but only Imperial dragons embroidered on the robes of the Emperor or his personal attendants could display five claws.

For all their ferocious appearance Chinese dragons were generally well-disposed toward humans. Only when provoked, by interference with their eggs for instance, would they retaliate. When displeased they usually caused storms and floods.

Kiang-su province. Even on windless days the seas in the area were so rough that no boat dared approach the island directly; at high tide, waves washed right over it. By night, a mysterious red light shone above the water, as bright as the sun and visible for a hundred miles around. Those who did venture close could hear what sounded like thousands of men felling trees and carting them away. And on clear nights it was even possible to make out the stumps of vanished forests on the island, razed to construct the abode of the Dragon King. In China, dragons had a pressing reason for choosing to live underwater: there they were safe from the terrible threat of centipedes, one of the few earthly creatures to strike fear in a dragon's heart.

In many other respects, the similarities between Indian nagas and Chinese dragons are too numerous and too exact to be ignored. Particularly striking is the resemblance between the functions of the four major types of naga and the four major *lung* dragons of China: the *t'ien lung* supports the mansion of the gods; the *shen lung* brings rain; the *ti lung* controls rivers; and the *fu-ts'ang lung* guards hidden treasures and deposits of precious metal. But just as the imported religion of Buddha was to take on uniquely Chinese characteristics, so nagas were adapted to suit Chinese tradition and belief. Fortunately, contemporary descriptions of dragons in China are so richly detailed that more is known about them than about the dragons of any other culture.

Apparently, dragons existed in the usual two sexes: "The male dragon's horn is undulating, concave, steep: it is strong at the top, but becomes very thin below. The female dragon has a straight nose, a round mane, thin scales, and a strong tail." If these sexual distinctions seem somewhat ambiguous, the dragon's processes of reproduction must seem even more so. According

Do dragons lay eggs?

to some authorities, when a pair of dragons mated, they transformed themselves into two small snakes. On the other hand, there is convincing evidence that dragons reproduce merely by laying eggs and, again, that "their eggs get life spontaneously," without mating.

While a few dragons laid their eggs on hillsides, most preferred to lay near water, in keeping with their aquatic nature. Dragons' eggs were commonly found alongside rivers, in the guise of beautiful stones; since some eggs did not hatch into dragons for a thousand years, they must surely have been prey to human avarice. The actual hatching seems to have been a spectacular affair. Much water running from the eggs was the first sign that the event was imminent. Thus alerted, the parents immediately gave tongue. The cry of

A horned Chinese dragon is called k'iu lung. *This is the third stage in the evolution from water-snake to winged dragon, a process that takes 3000 years in all. Some dragons, this one for example, have only three claws.*

the male made the wind rise, while the cry of the female made it abate; this had an alarming effect on local climatic conditions, which was not improved by the thunder and lightning, darkness, and torrential rain that accompanied the bursting of the eggs and the young dragons' ascent into the sky.

It was generally agreed that dragons' eggs were best left alone. One Chinese legend does suggest that this was not always the case: it concerns a woman who came across a clutch of five eggs in the grass near a river and decided to keep watch on them. These eggs soon hatched – but without the customary meteorological uproar – and the old woman guided the fledgling dragons to the river and let them go. As reward, the young dragons conferred on her the ability to foretell the future. In addition, whenever she went down to the river to wash her clothes, the fishes (subject, of course, to dragons) used to dance for her, providing a pleasing diversion from her chores.

Dragons usually hatched out in the form of small water-snakes or lizards,

The symbol of two interlocked curves represents the twin underlying principles of the Chinese Universe, Yin and Yang. Whether dragons derived from the Yang principle or from both was the subject of much learned debate in which the number of scales on a dragon was of great significance.

but rapidly and visibly began to grow towards maturity. Obviously speed of growth was essential, since the process of evolution amongst dragons took some time: "A water-snake after five hundred years changes into a *kiao*, a *kiao* after a thousand years into a *lung*, a *lung* after five hundred years into a *kioh-lung* (horned dragon) and after a further thousand years into a *ying-lung* (winged dragon)." This underlines not only the longevity of dragons, but their diversity. Recognized authorities divide them into four main groups:

"If a dragon has scales, he is called *kiao-lung*; if wings, *ying-lung*; if horned, *k'iu-lung*; if hornless, he is called *ch'i-lung.*" Some authorities recognize a fifth group: "Dragons that do not ascend to heaven are called *p'an-lung.*" Color was another aid to recognition: the *ch'i-lung* dragon, for instance, was red, white, and green, while the *k'iu-lung* was blue. But entirely black, or white, or red, or yellow dragons also existed, with the yellow type considered superior.

Since a lifetime in China that was both propitious and long might depend on accurate information about dragons, studies of them were highly detailed. A Chinese dragon normally had four legs, a long and sinuous body, with a snake-like tail but, other than in the case of the *ying-lung*, no wings. A dragon was said to have the following "nine resemblances": "The horns resemble those of a stag, his head that of a camel, his eyes those of a demon, his neck that of a snake, his belly that of a clam, his scales those of a carp, his claws those of an eagle, his soles like those of a tiger, his ears those of a cow." Alternatively the eyes are described as those of a rabbit. And usually, instead of wings, a dragon had on his head a large lump, the *ch'ih-muh*, that enabled him to fly; lacking this, a dragon clutched a small baton, called a *po-shan*, that provided the power of levitation.

Just as the number of heads on Occidental dragons reflected a cryptic significance, so the number of scales on a Chinese dragon was considered a matter of great importance. Some experts insisted that the scales of a true dragon numbered exactly eighty-one, equaling nine times nine. According to Chinese philosophy, the number nine is Yang, one of the two interlocking principles of the Universe; Yang represents Heaven, Light, Vigor, and Masculinity, while in contrast Yin represents Earth, Darkness, Passivity, and Femininity, and is associated with the number six. Other experts, arguing

Knowing your dragons could insure health and happiness

A five-clawed Imperial dragon decorates the back of the official robe of a eunuch of the court of Tz'u-hsi.

that dragons were not purely Yang but a combination of the qualities of Yang and Yin, put the number of scales at 117, made up of 81 imbued with Yang and 36 (six times six) with Yin. Under the chin of a dragon, certain scales were sharp and grew backwards; for a mortal to touch these scales meant certain death.

The number of claws possessed by a dragon also had a significance in the Chinese order of things: it was widely accepted that only Imperial dragons, like those embroidered on the robes of the Emperor himself, were depicted with five claws. Lesser dragons were accorded only four, or in some cases three.

The eyesight of dragons was acknowledged to be remarkable. They were credited with the ability to see (for what purpose is not explained) a mustard plant or a straw at a distance of one hundred miles. It was maintained by some that they did have their blind spots: "A dragon does not see stones" as "a man does not see the wind, fishes do not see the water, demons do not see the earth." The hearing ability of dragons is similarly an open question. Some experts claim them to be totally deaf, others to hear perfectly well through their cowlike ears; those lacking ears were said to use their horns instead. About those without either horns or ears, authorities are silent.

The origin of Chinese dragons was also a matter of great debate. Dragons of different colors were said to emerge from different inanimate substances. Yellow dragons, for instance, were said to come from yellow gold a thousand years old.

Some authorities argued that dragons mated like other animals and laid eggs from which their young were hatched. But others insisted that dragons were transformed snakes, animals, marine plants, or fish.

One reason given for wide variety amongst dragons was that not all were hatched from eggs; many originated by transformation from other animals. Some accounts insist that flying dragons were always the offspring of a particular kind of bird, *ying-lung* of a hairy quadruped called *mao-tuh*, *k'üh-lung* of a certain sea-weed, and so on. Snakes, too, could turn into dragons "since dragons and snakes are considered by the learned class to be related." And again, so could fish. In a river of Honan there is a stretch of rapids known as Lung Men, the Dragon Gate. Migrating fish gather below Lung Men and, according to legend, "those who can pass on upstream turn into dragons, while those who cannot bump their heads and bruise their cheeks." The proverbial saying, "The carp has leaped through the dragon gate" is an allusion to that phenomenon; it was a metaphor applied to those who successfully completed the gruelling examinations which were used to select entrants to the Imperial Civil Service, or to any form of literary success.

Divine Healing

For using dragons' bones first cook odorous plants; bathe the bones twice in hot water, pound them to powder and put this in bags of gauze. Take a couple of young swallows and, having taken out their intestines and stomach, put the bags in the swallows and hang them over a well. After one night take the bags out of the swallows, rub the powder and mix it into medicines for strengthening the kidneys. The efficacy of such medicine is, as it were, divine!

Lei Hiao

According to legend, several Chinese emperors were so well versed in dragon lore that they were able to make use of dragons to transport themselves and their courtiers around their kingdoms.

According to another tradition, dragons might emerge from inanimate matter; the yellow dragon was thought to be born from yellow gold a thousand years old, the blue from blue gold eight hundred years old, and red, white, and black dragons from gold of appropriate color, one thousand years old in each case. Supporting evidence did not accompany this theory.

The study of dragons was made even more complex by their ability to transform themselves at will. The only occasions when they were unable to effect such transformations were when they were being born, or when they were asleep, or when they were feeling either lustful or angry; this suggests that the process demanded a certain degree of concentration.

When assuming human form, dragons customarily chose to be either old men or beautiful young women. One such dragon-woman made herself a member of the Imperial court during the Hsia dynasty; she was said to devour men, a habit that may have gone unnoticed in an atmosphere of such intrigue. Among animals chosen as a disguise by dragons were fish, snakes, dogs, rats, and cows, whose ears of course were identical. But there were recommended methods of detecting such subterfuge: for example, a fish that emitted a five-colored light, or spoke in a human voice while being cooked, might certainly be suspected of being a transformed dragon.

A familiarity with dragons' likes and dislikes was considered just as valuable as an acquaintance with their metamorphoses. As an example, precious stones were known to give them pleasure, particularly the "Stone of Darkness," described either as a hollow stone with water inside, or as the vital essence of copper. Dragons were notoriously fond also of the roasted flesh of swallows, to the extent that people who had dined on this delicacy were ill-advised to travel across water immediately afterwards, lest an envious dragon should surface and attack them.

Among the things that annoyed or frightened dragons were the leaves of the *wang* plant (of which nothing is known, alas), the leaves of the *lien* tree (*Melia azederach*, or "Pride of India"), five-colored silk thread, wax, iron and, as noted earlier, centipedes.

Knowledge such as this was not merely precautionary; suitably applied, it could be used to exploit dragons in a variety of ways. Several eminent personages used dragons as a means of transportation. Huang Ti, the legendary Yellow Emperor and the god of architecture, rode on the back of a dragon, accompanied by more than seventy of his senior ministers. The remainder of his overstaffed cabinet did not manage to get aboard before the dragon flew away; in desperation they hung onto the dragon's whiskers, which unfortunately were pulled out by their weight, and they fell to the earth. Huang Ti also recruited a winged dragon to help him repulse an army of rebels. Kao Tsu of the Han dynasty, who reigned from 206 to 159 B.C., rode in a dragon carriage, as did the poet K'uh yuen, whose carriage was drawn by four flying

Roasted swallows are a favorite dragon delicacy.

Since there were no elephants in China, tigers were the only animals large enough to challenge dragons. But they were also frightened by centipedes, certain plants, wax, iron, and multicolored thread.

dragons; Si Wang Mu, the "Royal Mother of the West," who affected a carriage of purple clouds, was drawn by spotted dragons in nine different colors. About 800 B.C. another dragon towed the ship of the Emperor Ming Huang across a river and was rewarded by a gift of wine.

Occasionally, dragons were eaten. A king of the Hsia dynasty, circa 2000 B.C., fed upon dragons to make his reign propitious; it is not recorded if this was also retaliation against the dragon-lady who had been devouring his courtiers. Emperor Chao of the Han dynasty, 86 to 73 B.C., was fishing one day in the River Wei when he caught a white *kiao* dragon, resembling a snake but without any scales. "This is not a lucky omen," said Chao. Nevertheless, he ordered that the hapless dragon be prepared for his table. Its bones were blue and its flesh purple, but it proved to be savory and pleasant in taste.

As might be expected, the flesh of so remarkable a creature as the dragon proved more valuable as medicine than as food. In China the bones, teeth,

Because of dragons' notorious fondness for the flesh of roasted swallows, travelers who had eaten this delicacy were advised not to travel across water soon afterwards.

and saliva were, and to an extent still are, esteemed for their curative properties. By contrast, in the West dragons' blood was put to wide pharmacological use, while their bones and teeth were little used.

The medicinal role of dragons raised at least two acute philosophical questions: If dragons were of divine origin, surely then they must be immortal? And if they are immortal, how can they leave the remains used in medicine? The earliest Chinese medical work, *The Classical Work on Medicine* by the Emperor Shen Nung accepts the bones of dragons as belonging to dead dragons. The Emperor himself lived from 2838 to 2698 B.C. and his 140 years of life lend credence not only to his medical knowledge but to his belief in the curative qualities of dragon bones. Although his original treatise is lost, later medical writers quote extensively from it. They avoid the philosophical dilemma, however, by suggesting that dragons cast off both skin and bones much as insects and reptiles periodically discard their skins. A dragon could therefore discard his bones and other organs without suffering death.

Not all kinds of dragons were equally efficacious. According to a commentator of 500 B.C., one Lei Hiao: "Those which have five colors are the best, the white and yellow ones belong to the middle kind, and the black ones are the most inferior quality. As a rule those with veins lengthwise running are not pure, and those which have been gathered by women are useless."

In prescribing dragons' bones in medicine, the color was – to use the word in its exact original sense – quintessential. The five colors – blue, yellow, red, white, and black – correspond to the five felicitous plants, the five crystals, and the five types of mineral bole. In deciding on appropriate treatment all these correspondences had to be taken into account, as well as the compatibility of the color used with the affected organ. Blue corresponded to the liver and gall, white to the lungs and small intestine, black to the kidneys and bladder, yellow to the spleen and stomach, and red to the heart and large intestine.

Exacting procedures had to be followed in preparation. Some bones were slightly poisonous, and in preparation of these special care was essential. The use of iron utensils and any contact with fish had to be avoided. Bones had to be roasted over a fire until red hot and then rubbed into powder or, alternatively, soaked in spirits overnight, then dried again over a fire before being pulverized.

Powdered dragon bones were considered the effective cure for dysentery, gallstones, infantile fever and convulsions, boils in the bowels and internal

Powdered dragon bones - a magic cure-all.

Dragon evolution was a slow process. It took a thousand years for a water-snake to be transformed into this fire-spitting, horned lung *dragon.*

ulcers, paralysis of the legs, illnesses of pregnant women, and remittent fever and abcesses. Blowing powdered bones into the nose or ears stopped bleeding of those organs, and also alleviated the navel abcesses of babies. It was claimed that the strong Yang power of the bones overcame any Yin demons of illness that might infest a body. The possibility that dragons might incorporate both Yang and Yin was not discussed.

Dragon's skin glows in the dark

The cast-off skins of dragons were attributed miraculous properties, again on the grounds that they were powerfully imbued by the Yang principle. One anecdote concerns a man who, one dark night, saw a tree branch that glowed with a brilliant light. He broke it off and used it as a torch. The next morning, on examining the branch, he saw that its luminosity was due to the cast skin of a dragon. In size it resembled a cicada, but it had head, horns, claws, and tail. It was hollow inside, yet felt solid and, when tapped, produced the sound of a precious stone.

Dragons' fat could prove equally illuminating. With a rope of asbestos fibers as a wick, dragons' fat burned so brilliantly that it could be seen for a hundred miles. Fat could also render silk garments waterproof. It must be assumed that these apparently irrelevant benefits from dragons qualify, very loosely, as preventative medicine.

Dragons' teeth, however, had specific curative properties: they could be

Ethereal Dragons

When rain is to be expected, the dragons scream and their voices are like the sound made by striking copper basins. Their breath becomes clouds, and on the other hand they avail themselves of the clouds in order to cover their bodies. Therefore they are invisible. At the present day on rivers and lakes there are sometimes people who see one claw and the tail of a dragon, but the head is not to be seen. In the summer, after the fourth month, the dragons divide the regions amongst themselves and each of them has his territory. This is the reason why within a distance of a couple of acres there may be quite different weather — rain and a clear sky. Further, there are often heavy rains, and those who speak about these rains say: "Fine moistening rain is heavenly rain; violent rain is dragon rain."

used against complaints "that kill the vital spirit; when adults have spasms and epileptic fits, convulsions or madness, when they run as madmen and their breath is tied under their heart, so that they cannot breathe; further, the five kinds of fits, and the twelve kinds of convulsions of babies." They "quiet the heart and calm down souls," cure headaches, liver disease, melancholy, hot fever, madness (again), and possession by demons. Dragons' horns are counted to be equally useful.

The brain, and especially the prized "brain of a dragon a thousand years old," also cured dysentery. And the liver was sometimes recommended in difficult cases. The liver removed from a living dragon was particularly effective, and worth the trouble of obtaining it; this is vouched for by a writer who cites the case of one dragon that was forced by powerful charms to enter a jar of water.

The delightful ch'i-lin *appeared for the first time during the reign of the Chinese emperor Huang-ti (2697-2597 B.C.) according to the* Bamboo Chronicle *and was considered the noblest of all creatures in the animal kingdom. It represented peace, prosperity and good fortune, never ate living things and would not put a hoof on growing grass.*

The liver was then removed (how it was removed is left to the imagination) and given to the patient, who recovered promptly.

Another patient, a prince, was less fortunate. Desperate to acquire the coveted liver, he ordered that a dragon inhabiting a local pond be slain. Not only did this benign dragon supply the local people with rain in times of drought, but he also served as guardian of the castle. Hearing of the threat on his life, the dragon fled, after causing a terrible thunderstorm. Shortly afterwards, the prince's enemies successfully stormed the undefended castle. It is not recorded how the prince solved his own health problem.

The blood of Chinese dragons, red in some cases, black in others, was said to turn into amber when it entered the ground. Unlike Occidental dragons' blood, which served innumerable purposes, it seems to have had no other use. But amber, of course, was a highly prized commodity in China.

A flourishing trade in dragon spit.

Dragon saliva was also much sought after, again not as a medicine, but for the manufacture of perfume. "It is said that it can bind camphor and musk for several tens of years without evaporating. Further, it is said that, when it is burned, a blue smoke floats through the air. Last spring the saliva spat out by a

Some dragons had a lump on their heads known as the ch'ih muh, *which enabled them to fly. Others, without this organ, clutched a small staff called* po-shan *which helped them to levitate.*

herd of dragons appeared floating on the sea. The natives gathered, obtained and sold it, each time for 2000 copper coins." This so-called "saliva" sounds suspiciously like ambergris, a secretion of the sperm whale, which is still used in the manufacture of perfume. Since it, too, is usually found along sea-shores, the mention of "a herd of dragons" seems to suggest a case of mistaken identity.

Collection of this "dragon spit" apparently required skill and much patience. The people of Ta-shih used to watch the vapors arising from the sea for up to two or three years from the same spot. When the vapors vanished, it was a sure sign that the "dragons" that had been sleeping there had departed. The watchers went straight to the spot in their boats to gather the saliva left behind. In another account, the "dragons" lived in a whirlpool in the sea. Their saliva became hardened by the sun and was blown ashore in lumps by the wind. When fresh, the lumps were white, but gradually became purple, then black, with age.

More important even than the pharmaceutical effects of dragons was their influence on the weather. In dispensing rain, they were guided by instructions handed from the August Personage of Jade, Supreme Lord of the physical world, but they were allowed considerable latitude in deciding where, when, and in what quantities rainfall was to be allocated. It is not clear whether the particularly heavy rain known to follow conflicts between dragons was allocated or accidental. Certain observant if foolhardy persons claimed to have actually seen dragon battles taking place in the air.

A naked woman could cause violent 'dragon rain'.

It was thought possible, however, to manipulate the fall of rain by devious means. In times of drought, a dragon might be bribed with roasted swallows or prayers, or angered into causing a rainstorm by having poisonous plants, ashes, pieces of wood, stones, or tiger bones thrown into his pool. Alternatively, an attractive woman might be exposed, naked, on a hilltop, since dragons were notoriously lewd and fond of women. If they were then magically prevented from approaching the naked woman, their anger and frustration might be such as to result in rain. More decorous, but also more protracted and elaborate procedures were recommended if all else failed. These

The widespread use of dragons in decoration underlines their importance in Chinese life. Certain dragons were chosen to decorate specific objects because of their natural habits.

often involved the construction of artificial dragons of differing sizes and hues depending on the time of year, with which various complicated rituals were performed. Presumably such measures could be successful, since techniques had also to be devised for halting rain.

Close observation of dragons made it possible to predict forthcoming weather with an accuracy probably not much inferior to that achieved by present day technology. For example, in one region it was known that if the local dragon was seen to leave his den, drought was certain to follow. On occasion, the observation of dragon behavior was used for more general prediction; sightings of dragons could be interpreted as omens of good or ill, unrelated to the weather. If, for example, a traveler saw six dragons fighting one another, and if a blue or a yellow dragon was worsted, then the traveler could be certain that his journey would be fraught with hardships.

Another purpose to which dragons were put was the symbolic decoration of human instruments and artifacts. This involved a further classification of dragons into nine categories. The *p'u lao* dragon was carved on gongs, in recognition of the fact that it cried out loudly when attacked by whales. The *ch'iu niu* and *pi hsi* were carved on fiddles and stone tablets, on account of their respective liking for music and literature. The *pa hsia* appears at the base of stone monuments because it could support great weights, the *chao fêng* on the eaves of temples because it liked danger, and the *ch'ih wên* on the beams of bridges because it liked water. The *suan ni* always appeared on the throne of the Buddha because of its love of rest, the *yai tzŭ* on the hilts of swords because of its lust for blood, and the *pi han* on prison gates because of its quarrelsome nature.

Benevolent Chinese dragons are rarely slain.

Chinese dragons, then, may resemble those of the ancient Near East in many superficial and functional respects, but their mystical role is fundamentally different. First of all, Chinese dragons did not emerge from a creation myth, as did those of the Near East. Like Tiamat of the Babylonian Creation Myth, the Chinese dragon may be associated with water and weather but in no sense with the waters of primeval chaos; he may have a role in the irrigation of farmland but not in the violent establishment of the Universe, or in any vast mythical struggle between good and evil. In consequence, Chinese dragons rarely come into conflict with gods or heroes, and when they do it is by accident rather than by grand design. A few Chinese dragon-slaying legends do exist and when these do make a significant moral point it is an exceedingly subtle one. An example is the story of a would-be slayer of dragons who spent three years and all his wealth, a thousand ounces of gold, in painstaking pursuit of the skills required to kill dragons. But, until the day he died, he never had an opportunity to put those skills into practice. The moral of the story is that he would have been better to have followed the path of Tao to true enlightenment.

By observing the behavior of dragons, the weather or future events could be predicted. Dragons fighting each other might mean hardship on a journey.

Chinese dragons, perhaps reflecting the humane simplicity and unaggressiveness of China's prevailing religion, generally preserved a unique benevolence towards mankind not found in either the chaos-born dragons of Near Eastern myth or in the malevolent creatures who were to terrorize medieval Europe.

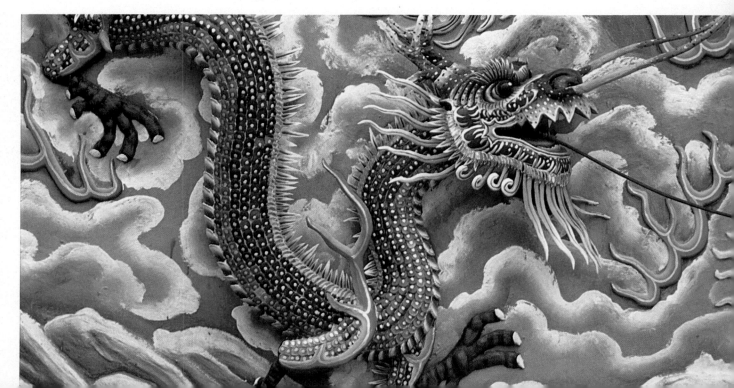

CLASSICAL

The most striking, and perhaps the most engaging, characteristic of the gods and goddesses of ancient Greece is their human frailty. The prominent inhabitants of Olympus had lively and distinctive personalities. They were mortals writ large, with all the human vices and virtues: the common inclination to get angry, petulant, jealous, or drunk. The roving eye of Zeus was the stuff of legend — he had after all more than fifty wives, mistresses, and lovers — as was the not unjustified jealousy of his first wife, Hera.

Despite their colorful personalities and their turbulent personal lives, the Olympians were not invented solely to provide entertaining legends. Their origins, too, lay in the incarnation of the process of Creation. In the beginning was Chaos who gave birth to, among others, Gaea, the Earth. She in turn gave birth to Uranus, the Sky, and by him bore Chronos, Time, and Rhea, Mother of the Gods. Chronos and Rhea, in the same incestuous family tradition, gave birth to the major Olympian gods, among them Zeus and his future wife Hera. And eventually Zeus seized power as the supreme god. This is, of course, a very much simplified account of the intricate and inbred origins of the major gods. The continuing tradition of promiscuity and incest was later to produce the minor gods and heroes of classical Greece.

As with the gods, so too with the monsters. As Gaea and Uranus were parents of the gods, so Gaea in her promiscuous fashion mated with Tartarus, the Underworld, to produce a complementary race of monsters, whose relationships were to prove as tortuous as those of the upper world. The children of Gaea and Tartarus turned out to be fearsome monsters, Echidna and Typhon. Echidna was half woman and half serpent, and perhaps as compensation for her mortality she was granted perpetual youth. Typhon, who is sometimes

PREVIOUS PAGE *Perseus, gallant Greek hero, rescues the distraught Andromeda from the ferocious sea monster with a fatal blow, delivering her from a most unpleasant end.*

A Vile Apparition

... up from his shoulders there grew a hundred snake heads, those of a dreadful dragon, and the heads licked with dark tongues, and from the eyes on the inhuman heads fire glittered from under the eyelids; from all his heads fire flared from his eyes' glancing; and inside each one of these horrible heads there were voices that threw out every sort of horrible sound.

After an initial setback the god Zeus overcame the terrifying monster Typhon with thunderbolts and imprisoned the dragon beneath Mount Etna.

identified with the Egyptian demon-god Seth, manifested himself as a powerful and destructive whirlwind, now known as a typhoon. In size and strength he surpassed all offspring of the lascivious Earth, towering over the mountains and occasionally brushing the stars with his head. From head to thighs he approximated human form, but sprouting a hundred dragons' heads and numerous wings; his lower limbs were huge coiling serpents. So awesome was he that when the gods first saw him they all fled to Egypt and hid, in the guise of various animals.

Zeus alone stood his ground against Typhon, first pelting the monster with the traditional thunderbolts and then closing in on him with a sickle made of adamant (a substance reputed to be as hard as a diamond). Typhon fled as far as Mount Casius in Syria, hotly pursued by Zeus, before turning at bay. In the ensuing struggle he gouged the earth with great furrows that were to become the riverbeds of the Near East. Grappling with Zeus, he managed to entwine him in his serpentine coils and to wrest the sickle from him. And with this, he severed the sinews of Zeus' hands and feet. The helpless god was imprisoned in a cave in Cilicia, guarded by a ferocious she-dragon, Delphyne. By means of a trick, two of Zeus' sons managed to reach their father and renew his sinews and his strength. Soon the reinvigorated god, riding the skies in a chariot drawn by winged horses, was again bombarding Typhon with thunderbolts. This time the chase led through Greece and across the sea to Sicily where, finally, Zeus cast Typhon into the Underworld and threw Mount Etna on top of him. The blasts of fire that issue from Etna to this day are attributable to the thunderbolts originally cast by Zeus. An alternative legend that eventually Typhon fled to Egypt and hid beneath a lake is dramatically less satisfactory and ecologically less plausible.

Whichever conclusion is chosen, the story conforms in its essentials to earlier creation myths. A ferocious monster, partly dragon and symbolizing chaotic storms, is confronted by a god. The god is a weather god and uses thunderbolts as weapons. After an initial setback, he triumphs and asserts his supremacy among the gods. The legend, for all its Greek elaborations, would

Only four days after his birth, the god Apollo slew the dragon Python with an arrow at Delphi, which was to become a center of the Apollonian cult.

Apollo kills the Python.

be acceptable in any part of the eastern Mediterranean area.

Another son of Zeus, the sun god Apollo, seems to have inherited his father's skill as a dragon slayer, a prowess he exhibited at a very early age. According to legend, a pregnant mistress of Zeus, Leto, was being persecuted by his jealous wife, Hera, and was forced to take refuge on the barren island of Delos in the Aegean Sea. The vindictive Hera, intent on destroying her, sent in pursuit of her a monstrous dragon, sometimes said to be the notorious she-dragon, Delphyne. Apollo, just emerged from Leto's womb, leapt to his feet and attacked the dragon with such ferocity that she retreated to her lair on the slopes of Mount Parnassus.

Four days after his birth, the precocious Apollo set out to seek a suitable place to establish a sanctuary for himself and his cult. He crossed to the Greek mainland and eventually, by chance, found himself high on Mount Parnassus where, from out of her lair in a rocky gorge, sprang the enraged Delphyne. Apollo let fly an arrow. In agony, "the monster lies shuddering: he rolls in the sand. He plunges into the forest and writhes on the ground, now here, now there, until the moment when, with poisonous breath, he exhales his life in a torrent of blood." Apollo contemptuously pushes the victim with his foot, saying, "Now rot upon the soil!" The change of gender in that quotation reflects a not uncommon conflict between versions of Greek legend. Initially the site of the battle became known as Pytho, and the dragon as Python, both deriving from the Greek word "to rot." Later the place was renamed Delphi, probably after Delphyne, and became one of the major centers of the Apollonian cult and the abode of the Delphic oracle.

Having dealt with the momentous establishment of the Olympians, Greek myth was later to concern itself with the affairs of lesser, but by no means less colorful, mortals. These are the heroes, many of them the result of Zeus' philandering with mortal women. Although human, these heroes were often to prove themselves superhuman. Despite the fact that Typhon had been put paid to by Zeus, and that Echidna had been slain by a hundred-eyed Olympian guardian named Argus, their incestuous coupling had produced a second generation brood of monsters for the heroes to contend with: there was Cerberus, the horrible watchdog of Hades, variously described as having between fifty and a hundred heads and a dragon's tail, or having three heads with many snakes writhing from his back; there was the enigmatic Sphinx, notorious for strangling her victims; there were some Vultures; and there were two monsters undoubtedly in the dragon class – the Chimera, and the leonine Hydra who lurked in the Lernean Swamp.

The Chimera lived in Lycia, a small province in southern Asia Minor, where she had been unwisely reared by a local chieftain. She was a fire-breathing monster, and identified as the volcano in the vicinity. The poet Homer describes her as being "a lion before, a serpent behind, she-goat in the middle"; it seems probable that the whole was more horrible than the parts.

The Chimera's fate was to a certain extent accidental. The hero Bellerophon fell foul of the King of Argos, who sent him to the King of Lycia unwittingly bearing a sealed letter directing that he should be killed on arrival. The Lycian monarch ordered Bellerophon to kill the troublesome Chimera, assuming the hero would die in the attempt. Bellerophon, however, had the advantage of

The awful fire-breathing Chimera, which was killed in Lycia by the Greek hero Bellerophon, but persisted as a volcano in the region.

ABOVE *The winged steed Pegasus on which Bellerophon was mounted when he killed the Chimera, first wounding the dragon with arrows and then dropping molten lead down its throat.*

OPPOSITE *The hero Herakles fights the multi-headed Hydra in the Lernean Swamp. As each head was struck off it was replaced by several more, but eventually he triumphed.*

being mounted on the winged steed, Pegasus. First, he was able to weaken the Chimera by shooting arrows at her from a distance; then, astride Pegasus, he flew over the monster's head and dropped lead, a proven antidote for dragons, into her gaping fiery mouth.

Another of Typhon and Echidna's dreadful children, the Hydra, was slain by another of Zeus' bastards, Herakles, better known under his Roman name, Hercules. The hero was one more victim of Hera's jealousy, having been driven mad by her and killed his own children. Partly to atone for this deed, Herakles went into exile in the service of his cousin, the King of Mycenae, who offered him the alternative of performing a series of formidable tasks, the celebrated twelve labors of Herakles. The second of these labors was to slay the Hydra.

The Hydra's lair was in the Lernean Swamp, the waters of which were unfathomably deep. The dragon had a dog-like or snake-like body and many leonine heads. The actual number of heads, ranging from seven through fifty to ten thousand, remains a matter of legendary dispute. But since the breath of the creature, and even the scent of its tracks, was lethally venomous, the number of heads was not of immediate importance.

Herakles, in a chariot driven by his nephew Iolaos, was guided to the Hydra's den by the goddess Athena. The hero forced the dragon to emerge by the tried-and-true method of raining down burning arrows on it. Then, holding his breath to avoid certain destruction, he tried to crush the several monstrous

COMBAT D'HERCULE CONTRE L'HYDRE DE LERNE.   Streit des Hercules, wieder die Lernische schlange.

Hercules's Combat with the Hydra.   Strydt van Hercules, tegens de slange van Lerna.

heads with his club. But whenever he struck off a head, two or three immediately grew to replace it (obviously making an initial count irrelevant). Herakles called on Iolaos' assistance. Iolaos set fire to an adjacent forest and, as Herakles destroyed each head, he scorched the stump to prevent regeneration. In this way the Hydra was finally slain.

Because he had had the help of Iolaos, this labor was discounted by the King of Mycenae and had to be compensated for by another, the theft of some golden apples from the Garden of the Hesperides. These much-prized apples had been a wedding present of the notoriously possessive Hera and were guarded in their garden below Mount Atlas by another of the monstrous Typhon-Echidna brood, Ladon, who, with a hundred heads, looked like his father and who "spake in many and divers sorts of voices." Herakles either killed Ladon, for all his immortality, or tricked him into falling asleep; in any case, he obtained the three apples.

As can be appreciated, Herakles was one of the greatest dragon-slayers of all legend. Sharing the precocity of many Greek gods and heroes, Herakles, like Apollo, began his lethal career early: while he was still an eight month old baby in his cradle, he strangled two giant snakes sent against him by the implacable Hera. Thereafter few dragons were safe. A final legendary exploit, one which was to serve as a model for both later dragon-slayers and for several Victorian painters, throws some light on Herakles' attitude to his profession.

It occurred when Herakles was passing through the city of Troy. Hesione, daughter of the local king, Laomedon, had had to be chained to a rock by the sea as a placatory offering to a ferocious sea-monster that had been terrorizing the city. Herakles offered to save her, and as reward was promised some horses of legendary power owned by the king. Inevitably Herakles slew the monster and rescued the girl, but Laomedon refused to keep his side of the bargain. So Herakles immediately sacked Troy, anticipating by several years the Trojan War described in Homer's *Iliad*.

The Trojan rescue by Herakles bears a marked resemblance to that of Andromeda by Perseus. Perseus, need it be said, was also a son of prolific

ABOVE *The hero Jason, in his first attempt to gain the Golden Fleece, is swallowed by the guardian dragon and then regurgitated. Helped by the goddess Athena, he eventually succeeds.*

ABOVE RIGHT *Cadmus, another heroic dragon slayer, confronts a dragon on the site of the city of Thebes. With the help of Athena, he also overcomes the monster.*

OPPOSITE *Another Greek hero Perseus, son of Zeus and a formidable slayer of dragons, comes to the rescue of Andromeda, who is about to be sacrificed to a local dragon.*

Zeus. With a considerable record against dragons, he was called upon by a king, possibly of Ethiopia, to despatch a dragon that had been sent to ravage the country by the sea god, Poseidon. To propitiate the monster and avert disaster, the king had been obliged to chain his daughter, the beautiful virgin Andromeda, to a rock by the sea in the customary sacrificial fashion. In passing, it might be inferred that dragons, whether Chinese or Greek, shared a penchant for pretty young women. Perseus fell in love with the victim at first sight and agreed to slay the dragon in return for her hand in marriage. He killed the monster and, in this case, the king stuck by the bargain. But unfortunately Andromeda had been betrothed already to one Phineus, who showed up at the wedding feast prepared to do battle for the bride. By chance Perseus had in a wallet, from an earlier encounter, the Gorgon's head, the eyes of which could turn a mortal to stone; Phineus was stopped in his tracks, eternally, and the wedding continued.

Another classical dragon-slayer of legend was Cadmus, no whit inferior because he was not a son of Zeus. Indeed, one of his most famous encounters occurred while he was attempting to recover his sister Europa from the rapacious clutches of Zeus. Following the directions of the Delphic oracle, he came to a locality that was later to become the site of the city of Thebes. The only water available thereabouts came from a spring sacred to Ares, god of war. This spring was guarded by the son of Ares, a ferocious dragon. Several of Cadmus' followers had been killed by the monster while trying to reach the spring before Cadmus himself slew it. The goddess Athena, who seemed often to be present at such battles, advised Cadmus to extract the dragon's teeth and sow them in the ground. When he did so, they sprouted up as a host of armed warriors. Craftily, Cadmus threw stones among them and, thinking each other responsible, they set on one another. Eventually all but five were slain, and these survivors became the founders of the noble families of Thebes. Subsequently, through circumstances too tortuous to relate here, Cadmus himself was turned into a serpent.

Athena kept half of the dragon's teeth obtained by Cadmus and eventually gave them to another Greek hero, Jason. He, too, sowed the teeth in the earth and saw a band of armed men springing up against him. Similarly, he provoked a melée by throwing stones and the warriors slew each other. This was, or course, a minor episode in the eventful life of Jason, most renowned for his quest for the Golden Fleece with his warriors aboard the *Argo*.

The fleece was guarded by an unsleeping dragon. According to some accounts, before he could seize the fleece, he was swallowed by the dragon and regurgitated, senseless; and he was said to be revived either by the goddess Athena or by the enchantress Medea, whom he later married. In the end, the dragon was either lulled to sleep by song or drugged by a magical

RIGHT *With a magic potion prepared by the witch Medea, Jason finally lulls the dragon to sleep, kills it and gains the Golden Fleece.*

As revenge against King Pelias, who sent Jason to fetch the Golden Fleece, Medea tricked his daughters into hacking their royal father to death and was later able to escape in a chariot drawn by dragons.

potion prepared by Medea and sprinkled on its eyes with a freshly-cut branch of juniper. This enabled Jason to make off with the Golden Fleece. Despite her aid, Jason was eventually to desert Medea for another woman. Enraged by jealousy she killed their children and fled to Athens in a chariot drawn by winged dragons.

Despite their reputation for irascibility, dragons in the west were often used to draw chariots, possibly because this might enhance the status of the chariot's passenger. For instance the hero Triptolemus, a favorite of the gods, was loaned a chariot drawn by two winged dragons which belonged to Ceres, the goddess of agriculture; from this he distributed wheat around the world. According to fable, the chariot survived and was later used by the Roman Emperor Julian during one of his military campaigns.

In both classical and Nordic mythology, volcanoes were attributed to the presence of dragons.

A 'drakon' is sighted over 200 feet long.

Wonders of Africa

According to some Classical authors, the "drakon" of Ethiopia grows to 180 feet in length; in fact many of them are so vast that "even grass grows on their backs," and people say that they kill and eat even elephants. In the words of the Roman poet Lucan (who was put to death by Nero in A.D. 65):

You also, the Dragons, shining with golden brightness, scorching Africa renders deadly. With wings you move the air on high and, following whole herds, you burst asunder vast bulls, embracing them in your folds. Nor is the elephant safe through his size; everything you devote to death, and no need have you of venom for a deadly fate.

It is interesting to contrast the dragon legends of classical Greece with those of the ancient Near East, from which, in part, they originate. Elements of creation myths do survive, as in the conflict between Zeus and Typhon. But the original myths usually involved only one monster, slain by a single god; in Greece many dragons arise, and are slain by equally numerous gods or heroes. While these proliferating encounters may seem to derive from the epic Zeus-Typhon conflict, their frequency seems to diminish their significance. While they may explain the founding of certain dynasties and cities, they no longer seem the key to the origin of the Universe.

Despite their increase, no ordinary mortal in classical Greece could expect to meet a full-scale dragon or giant serpent, any more than a humble serf in the European Middle Ages would expect to encounter the exiled serpent from the Garden of Eden or the monstrous dragons reserved for the likes of St. George. There seems to have existed a rigid hierarchy amongst monsters in the classical world that coincided with that classifying mortals, heroes, and gods.

Our word "dragon" derives from the Greek word *drakon* by way of the Latin *draco*. To the Greeks, *drakon* denoted either a very large snake or a genuine dragon, and when legend described Medea escaping in a chariot drawn by dragons, it seems unlikely that ordinary snakes were meant. When a contemporary account describes a *drakon* seven cubits long (ten and a half feet) this may well refer to a real snake such as a python, although they couldn't have been indigenous to Greece; but when the *drakon* grows to 140 cubits, and develops an appetite for whole elephants, the frontier between fable and fact has obviously been crossed.

Greek and Roman writers rarely attempted to define that frontier, possibly because it had little significance. After all, in ancient Greece creatures that obviously were ordinary snakes sometimes were considered to have inherited the magical and symbolic qualities that properly belonged to fabulous serpents and dragons. Sacred serpents that were neither immense nor ferocious seem to play a central role in several religious cults in Greece and elsewhere.

In Epirus, in northwestern Greece, for example, there was a sacred grove populated by snakes that were said to be descended from the Python slain at Delphi by Apollo. These were tended by a virgin priestess who, at an annual festival, brought them an offering of food. If the snakes took the food eagerly, the year ahead would be prosperous; if not, sickness and famine could be expected.

As among ordinary creatures, there was also a hierarchy among monsters. Lesser monsters were no match for the ferocity of a fully-fledged dragon.

In another such sacred grove, a *drakon* inhabiting a "vast and deep cavern" was not concerned with future prosperity. What it was expected to divine was of more personal importance to the "holy maidens" who came to offer it ritual food: "... and if they are virgins, the *drakon* accepts the food as sacred. Otherwise the food remains untasted because the *drakon* has divined their impurity ... ants crumble the cake from the deflowered maid into small pieces and transport them out of the grove, cleansing the spot. And the inhabitants get to know what has occurred and the maidens who came in are

According to classical mythology, the Greek goddess of the hunt had Aktaeon torn to pieces by his own hounds because he saw her naked. This illustration suggests that a dragon may have been involved in the dreadful deed.

OPPOSITE *Even on the sophisticated Roman walls of Pompeii, which was buried by the eruption of Mount Vesuvius, the dragon does not go unrecorded.*

examined, and the one who has shamed her virginity is punished." It may be assumed that the honor of serving as a priestess was not eagerly sought after in that community.

Other stories suggest that snakes were not invariably moralistic. During the time of Herod the King, for instance, tales were told of a *drakon* of enormous size that became enamored of a lovely girl: "He used to visit her and even slept with her like an ardent lover." But, of course, that kind of story is as old as history.

The myths of Greece were adopted virtually unchanged by Rome. Indeed it has been said that "Roman literature is Greek literature written in Latin" and, while this may be a little unfair, it is not totally untrue. While Zeus may have become Jupiter, Herakles Hercules, and so on, in their essentials the myths were little changed. Their Latin versions, circulated through the expanding Roman empire, were to permeate the cultures of parts of the world far distant from the sources in the eastern Mediterranean.

In the evolution of the mythical dragon, the major contribution of the classical era was to preserve a host of myths from a wide variety of sources

Roman dragon lore

More Wonders of Africa

Caius Plinius Secundus (known as the Elder Pliny) was a Roman man of letters who served as a high official under the Emperor Vespasian, and died while taking an imprudently close look at Vesuvius during the eruption which obliterated Pompeii. Pliny's *Natural History* rivals Aelianus in credulity and garrulity. He mentions a story so implausible that even the most credulous of later authors hesitated to repeat it:

Ethiopia produces dragons, not so large as those of India, but still twenty cubits in length. The Ethiopians are known as the Asachaei, among whom they most abound; and we are told that on these coasts four or five dragons are found twisted and interlaced together like so many osiers in a hurdle, and thus setting sail with their heads erect, they are borne along upon the waves, to find better sources of nourishment in Arabia.

RIGHT *Roman vestal virgins were required to minister to the needs of sacred serpents. Proof of virginity often depended on the reaction of the monsters.*

BELOW *With the advent of the Dark Ages, even dragons were depicted with a somber and more terrifying grotesqueness.*

within such awe-inspiring monsters as Typhon, the Python of Delphi, and the Chimera. But the multiplication of gods and demi-gods and heroes emerging from Olympus was reflected in a proliferation of dragons and monsters. Instead of being a unique monster, divine and mystical, living and dying at the sublime level of deities, the dragon emerged from the classical period as a member of a ubiquitous and somewhat mundane species. Despite its descent from the origins of the Universe, it was now essentially a mortal animal, no less familiar – and certainly no less plausible – than the giraffe or the elephant. By the beginning of the Middle Ages, the dragon haunted the periphery of everyday life and common religion in the Western world, having arrived by a different route at a position similar to that of the Indian nagas and the dragons of China, but destined to play a role much more malevolent and terrifying in men's imaginations.

MEDIEVAL

hen Rome's legions had been forced to retreat from northern Europe, the obscurity of the Dark Ages descended. The era between, say, the fifth and the ninth century A.D. is commonly assumed to have been one of barbarism and decline, but the light of civilization was not just snuffed out for two centuries and then suddenly relit at the beginning of the Middle Ages. It may have been dimmed during that violent period when hordes of Anglo-Saxons, Norsemen, Goths, and Franks swarmed in to fill the vacuum left by the collapse of Roman power, but where Roman order had prevailed, the essentials of civilization persisted; and Christianity from its Mediterranean heartland continued to extend its hold on men's minds, fostering literacy and art. In a figurative sense, the Dark Ages might seem to be a reenactment of a Creation myth:

PREVIOUS PAGE *The Middle Ages would eventually lead to the replacement of gods and heroes by saints and knights in the struggle against dragons. But the terrifying collapse of civilization into barbarism and violence was reflected in the image of dragons.*

Amidst so much chaos and darkness, men must have felt themselves at the mercy of monsters.

Dragons seemed to become more
awful, more savage, and more real.

OPPOSITE *The myths of the North reflect their earthly setting. Dragons often lurk in the cold sea or in gloomy lakes, to be glimpsed or imagined amid storms or fogs, an added peril in a harsh land.*

The Nordic giant Ymir spawns the first man and woman.

The dragons themselves assume the characteristics of the wild beasts that populate the Northern forests, no less savage and awesome than those that terrorized the ancient and classical worlds.

virtue, peace, and order confronted by evil, violence, and chaos are initially defeated but triumph eventually and emerge stronger than ever.

Myth feeds on obscurity, so inevitably the dragon, king of mythical beasts, not only survived but proliferated during the turbulent uncertainty of the Dark Ages. It too emerged stronger than ever, because the dragons of Near Eastern and Greco-Roman legend had been reinvigorated by interbreeding with the monsters of northern Teutonic myth. Whether human imagination spontaneously follows certain patterns, or whether Mediterranean legends filtered north by word of mouth, there are nevertheless some striking similarities between the northern and southern Creation myths.

At the dawn of time in the north only a yawning abyss stretched through space, another primeval chaos. From this, land and water emerged. Then came the creation of the first living being, the giant Ymir, who alone gave birth to a man and a woman. Several generations of giants and of humans followed until the universe was populated.

This established universe reflected the ecology of the northern scene. Its central feature was an enormous ash tree called Yggdrasil. This supported nine realms, that of gods, elves, dwarves, humans, the dead, and so on. Yggdrasil also had three roots that reached respectively into the worlds of Asgard, a walled city in which each god had a mansion; Midgard, where men lived; and Niflheim, which was the dark and gloomy underworld.

Niflheim was the lair of the first of the Nordic dragons, Nidhoggr. The "Dread Biter," as he was so vividly dubbed, spent his time gnawing at the root of the universal tree, threatening to destroy it. In this he was assisted by several lesser serpents and by an eagle, perched in the upper branches of the great ash, which sent encouragingly spiteful messages to the dragon by way of a squirrel called Ratatoskr. The destructive efforts of Nidhoggr and his allies were countered by beings called Norns, who repaired the tree daily by sprinkling it with gravel and water from a sacred well. The most serious threat to Yggdrasil would occur at the End of the World, but even then the primal tree would survive. The frustrated Nidhoggr would then fly off over the Hills of Darkness, bearing the bodies of the dead on his wings. One of his other gruesome habits, incidentally, was to clean the flesh off corpses.

Among the inhabitants of the world of Asgard was the fire-god, Loki, whose characteristics may seem familiar. Although a god, he was mischievous and unreliable. In the course of evolution of Nordic legend, he becomes progressively more demonic until, eventually, he kills one of his fellow-gods. As punishment the supreme god, Odin, has him bound and imprisoned

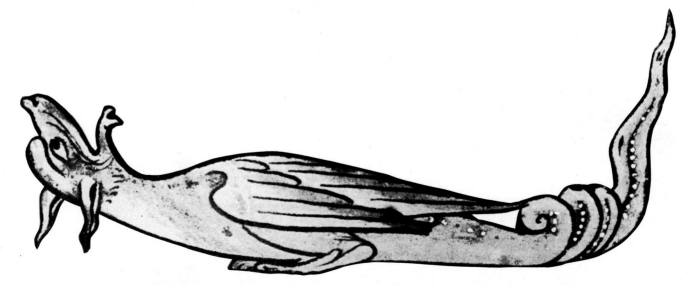

RIGHT *In Europe, dragons had a new and formidable foe to contend with – the Christian Church, with its hosts of guardian angels and indomitable saints.* OPPOSITE *Prayers and crucifixes were often to prove as devastating as swords and lances.*

beneath the earth, and thereafter his struggles to get free cause earthquakes and volcanic eruptions. The legends of Seth and of Typhon are immediately brought to mind.

A further parallel between Loki and the Greek Typhon is that both fathered broods of monsters almost as terrifying as they themselves. Loki's offspring comprised the dreadful wolf Fenrir, a monster called Hel, and the Serpent of Midgard, which was the world of men. All three had to be restrained: Fenrir was chained by magic fetters; Hel had to be cast down into the underworld of Niflheim, where she was to become queen; and the Serpent of Midgard was thrown into the depths of the ocean "where it now lies, completely ringing the world. For the old dragon so increased in length and girth that he came full circle and now grips the end of his tail in his jaws."

Despite this banishment, the Serpent of Midgard was not immune from attack. Indeed, another Nordic god, Thor, was both intent and destined to kill the monster. Thor, who may be assumed to be a son of Odin, is described as having red hair, a red beard, and red eyebrows. He was the god of thunder and wielded a hammer called Mjölnir that emitted thunderbolts and lightning. He rode across the sky in a chariot drawn not by a pair of winged dragons but by a couple of goats. This final incongruous note seems to typify the farcical air of many of Thor's exploits, including his initial attempt to kill the Serpent of Midgard.

Thor's chariot is drawn by goats

Thor's second, and fatal, confrontation with the Serpent is devoid of comedy, however. It is predicted to take place during Ragnarök, the epic Twilight of the Gods and end of the world, a series of events described in details as fearsome as those of the Apocalypse. Similarly, image is piled upon image to create a vivid and horrifying picture of the final cataclysm, but with images appropriate to its northern setting. First there will come three winters during which the world will be embroiled in war; then the Monstrous Winter equal in length to three normal winters but unalleviated by summer. The sun and moon will be swallowed, and the mountains will shudder. The awesome ship Naglfir, built with the nails of dead men, slips its moorings;

the wolf Fenrir, rabid offspring of Loki and brother of the Serpent of Midgard, breaks loose from its magic fetters. The great Serpent lashes to and fro in the ocean, flooding the land with tidal waves; he "blows such clouds of poison that he sprinkles all the earth and sky; he would make your blood run cold as he comes on the other side of the Wolf."

The heavens split asunder to reveal the advancing armies of terror and destruction. The gods sally forth against them, led by Odin, with Thor at his side. But soon Odin is devoured by Fenrir, and although Thor manages to slay the Serpent of Midgard, he himself is overwhelmed by the monster's toxic breath and staggers back only nine paces before falling dead in his tracks. The widespread bloodshed that follows is ended by the fire-giant Surtr, who spews flame over the scene, finally consuming both world and heaven. It might seem the end of all things, but after a time, it is predicted, the earth will rise again, green and fair, from the sea. A few gods will have survived, or will be raised from the dead, and will return to the heaven of Asgard. A man and a woman, too, will have escaped oblivion. And so the universe can begin again.

Many elements in this legendary sequence must seem familiar. Like Tiamat and other "world serpents," the Serpent of Midgard dwells beneath the ocean, encircles the earth with his coils and causes storms by his writhing. Thor, armed with thunder and lightning, conforms admirably to the finest traditions of dragon-slaying weather gods; he measures up to Marduk and Baal, to Indra, the Hittite slayer of Illuyankas, and even to the mighty Zeus.

There is one element that is markedly different, however: in most legends of Mediterranean origin, the slaying of the dragon is a stage in the creation of the world, whereas in this Nordic myth it occurs at the end. Oddly enough there is a resemblance between this purely pagan myth and the Christian vision of the Apocalypse provided by St. John the Divine in his Revelations, where the dragon is cast down as the world ends and "a new heaven and a new earth" replace it. While it seems unlikely, it is not impossible that one of

these myths might have influenced the other. Nevertheless the Nordic myth remains unique in suggesting that the cataclysm of the Ragnarök is part of an eternal cycle of creation, destruction, and re-creation. The new heaven and new earth (to say nothing of the hell) of Christianity is intended to last forever. Which is preferable is a moot point.

Nordic myths, like those of classical Greece, allow mortal heroes as well as gods to try their hand at slaying dragons. The best known of such mortals

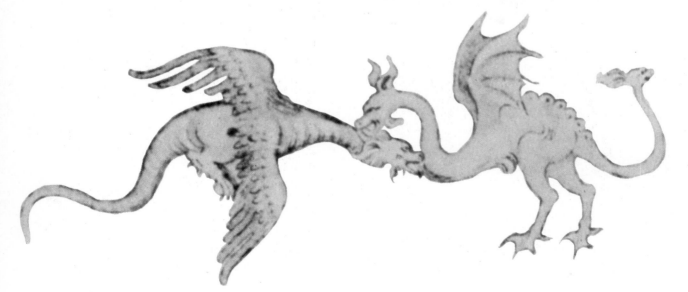

As this carved rune-stone suggests, there was little peace between the strange monsters of Nordic mythology.

was Sigurd, or Siegfried, whose epic disagreement with the dragon Fafnir won him a form of immortality in Richard Wagner's opera-cycle, "The Ring." Fafnir might well be described as a dragon by choice: he began life as a giant, killed his own father to acquire a treasure, and then assumed the shape of a dragon to guard his ill-gotten gains. There are several versions of Sigurd's dealings with him: in one, Sigurd, in the best heroic tradition, slays the dragon to rescue a maiden; in another, he craftily conceals himself in a pit to strike the dragon from beneath; and in yet another, he acquires invincibility by the distasteful process of bathing in the dragon's blood.

In Scandinavian but not in Teutonic legend, Sigurd roasts the dragon's heart over a fire, accidentally burns a finger while testing the progress of the barbecue, puts his finger in his mouth, and so inadvertently tastes the dragon's blood, which immediately instils in him an understanding of the language of birds. This gift of avian tongues seems to have been highly prized in legend. It will be recalled that both Greeks and Indians were glad to eat parts of snakes, dragons, and nagas to attain it.

Sigurd was not alone in the heroic profession of dragon-slaying. The famous Old English alliterative epic *Beowulf*, probably composed in the seventh or eighth century A.D., records the slaying of dragons by Sigurd's father, Sigmund, and by Beowulf himself. In both incidents, the dragon was a guardian of great treasure, but Beowulf was not to profit from killing the monster because in the course of the battle he was fatally poisoned. Sigurd's exploits are again echoed in the Danish *Hrolf's Saga*. Here a certain Bothvar put paid to a horrible winged dragon, but it was one of his associates who drank the dragon's blood and ate its heart, thereby becoming brave and strong. Celtic heroes were not to be outdone by those of the north. The legendary Irish hero Finn MacCumhaill, while a redoubtable slayer of dragons, obviously had no appetite for them. Nevertheless, while cooking a monster salmon he burned his thumb, put it in his mouth, accidentally tasted the magic fish, and so acquired great wisdom. Whether wisdom extended to greater skill in cooking is not mentioned.

Most early Nordic dragons seem to have been huge and largely aquatic. Winged dragons, on the other hand, appear to have been relatively unusual in the more northerly parts of Europe — in Scotland, Scandinavia, and northern Germany, despite their prevalence further south. It could be that the overcast unstable weather of the area discouraged the notion of flight. But it is more significant that the areas overflown by winged dragons coincide roughly with the areas of Roman occupation and influence. As it happened, in the latter days of the Roman Empire one of the common military standards was the *draco*, a representation of a winged dragon. It seems quite possible that this emblem, adopted by the Romans from the conquered peoples of the Empire's eastern provinces, shaped the evolution of the dragon's image in the west. Eventually the *draco*'s wings were to sprout on the dragons of the north.

And so there emerged from a diversity of cultures and mythologies a dragon that was to grip and terrify the imagination of Europeans during the Middle Ages and beyond. Its deadly breath and association with water and storms may have been drawn from the Serpent of Midgard; its wings either from the Nidhoggr or the Roman *draco*; its possession of treasure from the legend of Sigurd and Fafnir. As a descendant of the bloodcurdling Nidhoggr, it was little wonder that this dragon invariably suggested menace, evil, and

The epic violence of Sigurd's battle with the Nordic dragon Fafnir is re-created by a craftsman in the wood of an ancient Scandinavian portal.

death; gods and heroes were in continual demand to challenge and destroy it. While its most immediate ancestors were obviously the creatures of Northern legend, however, it is possible to discern in them a far more ancient and distant ancestry, possibly traceable to the Near East, and even to the primeval clash between Tiamat and Marduk. If no actual dragon had been involved in the process of Creation accepted by Christians, a serpent had played a part in man's fall from grace into a world where he was forever threatened by evil and violence and chaos. The dragon, born out of violence and chaos, served as a perfect image of such perils.

Christian morality pervaded life and thought in the Middle Ages. The moral significance of animals, whether mundane or mythical, was studied more closely than their physical characteristics. The medieval attitude is well summed up by the twelfth century scholar, Alan of Lille:

Every creature in the world
A book and picture is for us
And like a mirror too.

Sigurð & the Dragon Fafnir

Now Sigurd and Regin, Fafnir's brother, rose up to the moors, to the track along which Fafnir used to crawl when he went to drink, and the crag he lay on to get at the water when he drank was said to be thirty fathoms high.

"You told me," said Sigurd then, "that this monster was no bigger than any serpent but his tracks look very big to me."

"Dig a pit," said Regin, "and sit in it, and when the dragon comes crawling to the water, stab him to the heart and so destroy him."

So Sigurd rose up the moors and Regin went off in a great fright. Sigurd dug a pit to conceal himself in, and other pits for the monster's blood to run into.

And when the dragon crawled to the water, the earth shuddered and the land all around shook. He breathed out poison all over the path ahead. But Sigurd was neither frightened nor dismayed. When the dragon crawled across his pit, Sigurd thrust in his sword under the left shoulder, and it sank in up to the hilt. Then he leaped out of the pit, wrenching back his sword, and getting his arms bloody right up to the shoulders. And when the huge dragon felt its death wound, it lashed with its tail and head, shattering everything that got in its way. And then Fafnir died.

Then Sigurd cut out the dragon's heart with the sword called Ridill. Regin then drank the blood of his brother Fafnir and said to Sigurd:

"Do something for me — it's a small matter. Take the heart to the fire, roast it and give it to me to eat."

Sigurd went and roasted it on a spit. And when the juice sputtered out he touched it with his finger to see whether it was done. He jerked his finger to his mouth, and when the blood from the dragon's heart touched his tongue he could understand the language of the birds.

Saga of the Volsungs (13th century)

ABOVE *Another vision of the Apocalypse from a fourteenth-century German altarpiece. The woman clothed in the sun, with a crown of twelve stars, is threatened by a dragon.*
OPPOSITE *St. Martha of Bethany, patron saint of cooks and housewives, subdues the frightful Tarasque on the banks of the Rhône by sprinkling it with holy water.*

The fearful image of a dragon could drive home a point of morality far more vividly and forcefully to simple churchgoers than any argument based on hair-splitting theology. But dragons were often used to illustrate doctrinal issues more baffling and awe-inspiring than dragons themselves. The seven-headed dragon of the Apocalypse, for instance, was taken to represent not just evil but, more specifically, the persecution of the True Church by its foes. Body, tail, and each of its seven heads had a special significance. The body represented all the sinners; the tail, fittingly, the Last Tribulation. The

A Chronology of Dragons

1170
In the seventeenth year of Henry II, there was seen at St. Osythes (Essex) a dragon of marvellous bigness, which, by moving, burned houses.

1177
In this year many dragons were seen in England. The same year a great wind blew shortly before Christ's Nativity, and the sun eclipsed.

1222
In this year there were tumultuous riots in the city of London. Dragons were seen flying through the air. At the feast of St. Andrew there was terrible lightning and thunder; houses and trees were blown down, and there were bad floods.

1233
On the 8 daie of Aprill, in the parts about Hereford and Worcester, there appeared foure sunnes in the element, beside the naturall sunne, of red colour ... The bishop of Hereford and sir Iohn Monmouth, knight, and manie others behold this wonderful sight, and testified the same to be most true. And after this there followed the same yeare in those parts cruell warre, slaughter, terrible bloodshed & a generall trouble through England, Wales, and Ireland. About the same time, to wit, in Iune, in the south part of England neere to the sea coast, two huge dragons appeared fighting in the aire, and after a long fight the one overcam the other, and followed him, fleeing into the depth of the sea, and so they were seen no more ... Moreover in this yeare great variance and strife rose betwixt the king and his barons ...

1274
In the vigil of St. Nicholas there was an earthquake and thunder and lightning; a fiery dragon and a comet terrified the English.

1395
In Aprill, there was seene a fierce dragon in manie places of England; which dreadful sight as it made manie a one amazed, so it ministred occasion of mistrust to the minds of the marvellous, that some great mischeefe was imminent, whereof that burning apparition was a prognostications.

1499
In ... the 26 day of May, there came a Dragon to the City of Lucerne, which came out of the Lake through Rusa, down along the River, many people of all sorts beholding the same.

1532
In the year 1532, in manye countries were dragons crowned seene flying by flocks or companies in the ayre, having swines snowtes; and sometimes were there seen foure hundred flying together in a companie.

Monastic Annals, Holinshed, Topsell, Brand

Seven heads, ten horns, bear's feet and a lion's mouth . . .

seven heads stood, in order, for Herod; Nero; Constantine Arianus, son of Constantine the Great and a supporter of the Arian heresy that split the early Church; the Persian King Cosdroe, under whose reign Persia came "into the hands of Saracens and Mahomet"; Saladin, "one of the kings of Babylon"; and lastly, "that Great Tyrant" whose coming is foretold in the Apocalypse. Sometimes, for reasons of theological expediency, the second head represented an alternative set of heretics; or the fourth head, Mohammed; or the seventh, Emperor Frederick II, who was excommunicated by Pope Gregory IX in 1227.

Even if this symbolic elaboration was far above the heads of most devout laymen, their consciousness of the dragon was heightened by other means during the Middle Ages. The decoration of churches was encouraged because it helped priests to illustrate their sermons and to convey to a largely illiterate congregation a vivid impression of the Church's vision of the universe. The imaginative zest and skill of medieval craftsmen and artists, inspired by legend and folklore that was more often pagan than Christian in origin, was difficult to curb, as medieval churches and works of art still demonstrate. Dragons writhed with fearsome brilliance across murals and, later, high in stained-glass windows. Gargoyles and griffins and other terrible monsters

Dragons, and even specific parts of dragons, represented some aspect of the Church's dogma and the wordly and spiritual enemies of the faith.

Pictures and murals of dragons in medieval churches were intended to inform as well as intimidate the faithful. Each kind of dragon had an allegorical significance.

glowered menacingly down on worshipers from eaves and porticoes every time they came to mass. If they were not made more devout and moral by these reminders of the perils of the world, they must certainly have been excited by a mixture of awe and wonder that helped divert them during the tedious enactment of the Mass. Many of us today can recall how we endured the boredom of childhood Sundays by fantasizing on the allegorical art of churches. Swarms of worldly tourists still circulate through the medieval churches to gaze in awe at the fabulous beasts dreamed up centuries ago by simple craftsmen.

The dreams of such craftsmen, however, were not colored only by the legends of their region or of Europe. The means of travel, of trade, and of exchanging ideas had continued to improve and this tended to enhance rather than diminish belief in dragons. As in Pliny's day, India and Ethiopia were thought to be heavily populated by such monsters on the grounds that dragons, as agents of evil, felt more at home in pagan countries than in Christian Europe. "Many other bestes peryllous and terryble ben ther in Ynde, as dragons, serpentes and other dyverse beestes whiche have feet, heedes and taylles dyverse ... wormes ther growe there, whiche have two armes so longe and so dyverse that they bete and slee the Olyphaunts."

Since much of medieval dragon lore was legendary, and in the oral tradition of folk tales, many of the encounters between dragons and heroes, saints and martyrs are preserved only in pictorial form, where reality is too often defeated by wishful imagination.

The finer points of medieval theology and the concerns of religious politics were difficult to convey to a largely illiterate laity. Since dragons in their various guises provided limitless scope for free interpretation, they were used extensively in both the Christian and Islamic worlds to illustrate in vivid terms the perils that awaited those straying from the path of righteousness and the enemies that beset the true faith.

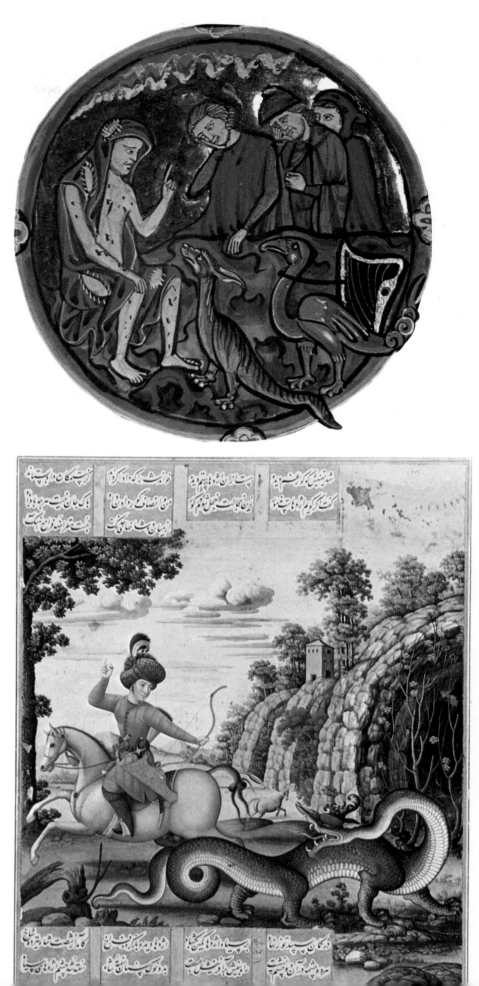

Throughout the Middle Ages dragons and Christianity complemented each other. The power both of dragons and of faith was mutually enhanced (RIGHT AND OPPOSITE). Sailors (ABOVE), always more subject to hazard than the rest of men, assumed in adding a dragonesque figurehead that if you cannot be sure of beating sea-dragons you might as well pretend to join them.

Huius aute et aliorū prius paul⁹ pīntus w
ma fugiēs maria trāsuut z uastissimā hēmū
peait secus mare rubzum p̄ quod tēpus ā́tonī
melioz̄ se lxiemū m colere edocetur i sompnio

So large did dragons loom in popular imagination in the Middle Ages that spurious accounts and pictures of them were fabricated for a ready market. Since knowledge of dragons was sketchy at best, imagination knew no bounds.

One of the most prolific contributors to the medieval bestiary was Sir John Mandeville, whose *Travels* are based on fourteenth century voyages to the East. For example, he describes the desert around the Tower of Babylon as being "... full of dragons and great serpents, and full of dyverse venymous beasts all about." Obviously time and catastrophe had not diminished Babylon's attractions as a resort for dragons.

But what is most fascinating about Sir John Mandeville is the fact that he was as much a fable as the beasts he described; while a Sir John Mandeville may have existed, he was not the author of the *Travels*. The entire work was fabricated from the accounts of several travelers by a literary ghost whose true identity remains a mystery. This practice of concocting literary works and falsely attributing them to notable people was quite common in the Middle Ages. The more eminent the name attached to such spurious works, the more widely it would be read and believed. The Greek philosopher

The so called Travels of Sir John Man-deville, *concocted from several travelers' tales and falsely attributed to a real person, included among many other fables one about a dragon that assumed the form of a damsel and attempted to lure a knight into her lair. His rectitude enabled him to live and tell the tale.*

Aristotle was much favored by ghost writers. The belated appearance of posthumous work by him was explained by the fable that he had had certain writings buried with him and that these were now being disinterred and circulated. It could be safely assumed that none of Aristotle's descendants would appear to challenge the works' authenticity or to claim copyright.

The great winged serpents which basked in the parched deserts of the East were just as menacing to imaginative fourteenth century travelers as the tales of writhing sea creatures which had filled the Nordic sagas.

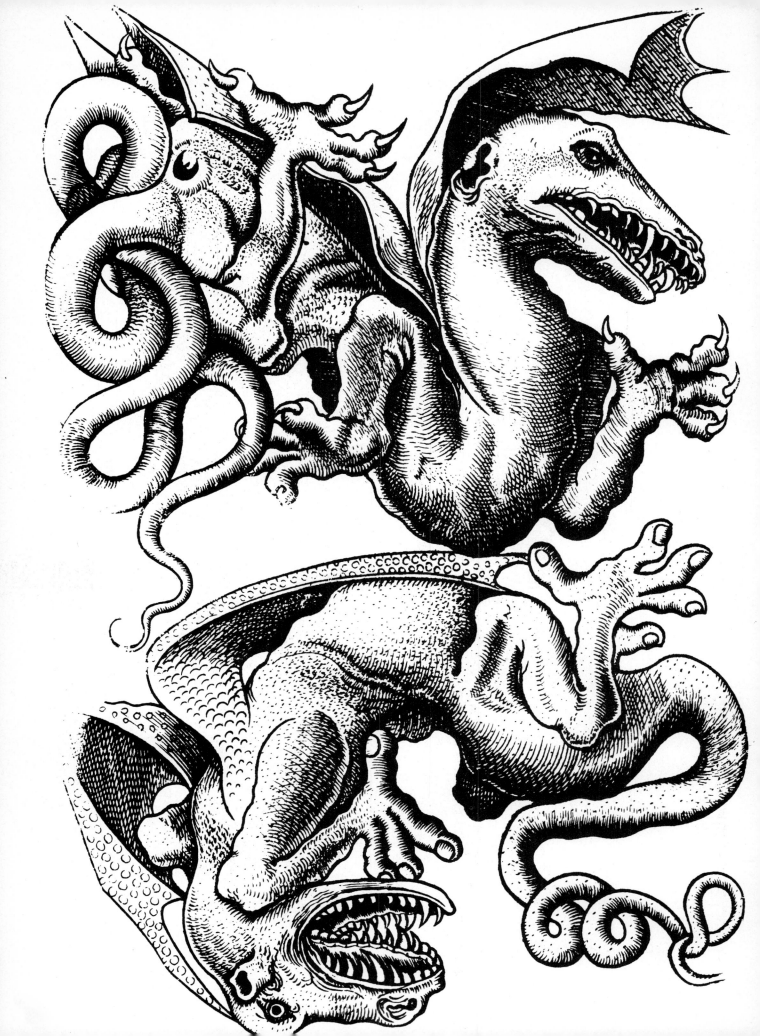

ABOVE *To have confronted a dragon of some sort, and the bigger and more horrifying the better, became the mark of a true gentleman at arms. It was considered good form to do so single-handed.*

OPPOSITE *Medieval travelers were beset by incredible hardships, not least of which were the hazardous encounters with fantastic creatures said to lurk in every swamp or mountain pass along the route.* BELOW *The extraordinary begetting of Alexander.*

The self-effacing "pseudo-Aristotle," as he is called by today's scholars, did not allow himself to be restrained by the austere cerebral cast of his model's authentic writing; indeed, medieval readers must have been amazed by the imaginative flair of Aristotle's latterday work. One anecdote from it gives the flavor: Apparently, during the reign of Philip of Macedon, whose son Alexander the Great was somehow sired by a dragon, a mountain pass in Armenia became impassable. Every traveler who had attempted to cross died from the poisonous air. Puzzled by the source of this pollution, Philip appealed for help from another classical genius, Socrates. Socrates, by means of magical skills, raised a tower as high as the mountains, and fixed on top of it a steel mirror; in later versions the mirror is replaced by an "Optick Philosophical Glasse," some early form of telescope. By whichever means, Socrates was able to perceive that the cause of the trouble was a couple of dragons disporting themselves in the pass and fouling the air with their breath. With this diagnosis made, the problem was solved by sending in two heroes in airtight armor to slay the dragons. The use of a mirror seems to suggest that only the direct gaze of a dragon was fatal.

Even the most truthful observer could contribute unwittingly to the popular belief in dragons. Marco Polo, traveling in thirteenth century Caragian, which is now the Chinese province of Yünnan, wrote of ferocious "serpents" ten paces in length and as thick as a cask, with two squat forelegs near the head, claws like those of a lion, enormous heads, eyes "bigger than loaves" and a mouth that could swallow a man in one gulp. By allowing for some exaggeration, it may be deduced that these formidable beasts were in fact

RIGHT *Possibly miscegenation between a lugubrious dragon and a sacrificial virgin produced this curious mutant.*

BELOW *If contemporary illustrations are to be believed, many fabulous beasts were of modest size and quite beautiful to behold. It seems unlikely, as some pictures suggest, that they often attained the status of domestic pets.*

crocodiles. The absence of a second pair of legs may be attributed either to the fact that crocodiles commonly lie half-submerged in the shallows of rivers, or to the fact that observers confronted by an advancing crocodile rarely take time to scrutinize the whole length of the brute. For all his

The general run of dragons were grotesque, cumbersome and rarely conformed to any standard physical pattern. Their variety was the despair of scholars at the time.

accuracy of description, Marco Polo was at the mercy of his illustrators. The artist illustrating one version of the explorer's journal simply showed the serpents of Caragian as dragons, since as a European these were more familiar to him than crocodiles; he even added to his illustration wings and other dragonesque accessories that Marco Polo had omitted to mention. And so, subsequently, the great explorer who had never used the word "dragon" was cited in support of the common belief that winged dragons were indigenous reptiles of the Orient.

During the Middle Ages, familiar and ancient legends were continually being embroidered. It was claimed, for instance, that so great was the traditional antipathy between elephants – the "Olyphaunts" cited earlier – and dragons that when elephants saw a man assailed by a dragon, they would run to his aid. There is no record of what the Egyptian god Seth, elephantine at first and later a dragon, might have done in such circumstances.

Such questions were the subject of intense debate between medieval scholars. It was generally conceded that most dragons reproduced by laying eggs. But a minority view that Egyptian dragons brought forth their young like mammals, and had breasts with which to suckle them, raised a great deal of controversy. As did the assertion that dragons were the offspring of matings between eagles and she-wolves.

If less debatable as a topic, the feeding habits of dragons raised more practical problems. Their voracious appetite for humans and domestic animals was indisputable, and saints were kept busy slaying dragons who were exorbitant in their demands for a daily supply of cattle, sheep, or maidens. A dragon, kept as a pet by one of the popes, was said to consume six thousand people a day. Since Rome itself could not sustain such a population drain for long, it is possible that the Pontiff imported heathens for the purpose. Another dragon acquired a taste for the blood of a young girl and could only be terrorized out of the habit by the flourishing of a religious relic; of course, it was realized later that the dragon was none other than Satan in one of his many disguises.

Dragons had a particular liking for doves, which posed for them a unique dilemma. Doves in India tend to frequent the branches of the Perindeus tree, for the succulent fruits of which they, in their turn, have a particular liking. Dragons may encircle such trees and await their chance of an unwary dove, but unfortunately dragons happen also to be extremely afraid of the Perindeus tree, to the extent that "if the shadow of the tree falls to the west, the dragon betakes himself to the east, and if the shadow comes to the east, he flees to the

A pontiff's pet devours 6000 souls a day.

Since dragons were commonly considered creatures of the Devil, the mischief they might turn to was never a matter of surprise.

Monster Most Foul

There was in Paris a lady of high rank who had lived a very abandoned life, and had died in her sins. Being a Christian, and not excommunicated, she was buried in consecrated ground; but that same night a hideous and gigantic dragon came from a desert to Paris, hollowed out a great hole for his lair, and began to feed on the dead body. It did not devour it all at once, but returned again and again. As the breath of the monster infected the air, those dwelling near the churchyard were so greatly alarmed that they were forced to leave their houses, and St. Marcel was beseeched to come to the rescue. Armed with arrows and spears, he went to the churchyard; and when the dragon approached him, he knocked it three times on the head with his cross. Then, throwing his cloak around the monster's neck, he led it four miles beyond the city gates and said to it: "Either promise never again to quit this spot, or I will cast you at once into the sea!" The dragon made the required promise, and was never again seen in the vicinity of Paris.

Brewer, Gregory of Tours

It was believed that the Devil himself would sometimes assume the form of a dragon and wreak his vengeance on the homes of good Christians.

west." No reason is given for this irrational fear in dragons, but it can be assumed that the doves took full advantage of it.

There were other reasons why dragons were not welcome as local fauna. Whole tracts of countryside could be rendered uninhabitable and birds made to fall out of the sky by the very breath of a dragon. This problem was most acute in Ethiopia, where the great heat tended to make the dragons more poisonous than they were elsewhere. In addition, dragons deliberately ate poisonous herbs "so that if they bite after them, many not knowing the cause of the poyson, and seeing or feeling venom by it, do attribute that to his nature which doth proceed from his meat." It seems doubtful that such knowledge would have counted for much as a final consolation.

Given such unwise eating habits, it is not surprising to learn that dragons were occasionally ill. Sometimes they cured themselves by eating the herb "balis," which was said to be efficacious enough to restore the dead offspring of dragons to life. Blindness, apparently a common affliction of dragons, could be cured by rubbing the eyes with fennel, or by eating it. One dragon, however,

Mercy from on High

St. Simeon, it is recorded, astonished the whole Roman Empire by the extent of his mortifications. He first joined a monastery so austere that the monks were permitted to eat only one meal a day: Simeon ate but once a week. The head of the community requested him to be less ostentatious in his privations, so Simeon left the monastery. After many years of diverse self-inflicted penance, he hit on the idea for which he is best remembered, and which made him known as St. Simeon Stylites (St. Simeon of the Pillar). He first stood on top of a pillar six cubits high (9 feet) for four years. Not satisfied with this, he moved to a second pillar of 12 cubits (18 feet) for three years, to a third of 22 cubits for 10 years and, finally, to a pillar of 40 cubits (60 feet) where he spent the remaining 20 years of his life.

Near this last pillar was the lair of a dragon, so very venomous that nothing could grow near the mouth of his cave. This dragon met with an accident: he had a stake in his eye and, coming all blind to the saint's pillar, he placed his eye upon it for three days without doing any harm to anyone. Simeon ordered earth and water to be placed upon the dragon's eye; when this was done, the stake — a cubit in length — immediately came out. When the people saw this miracle, they glorified God, and ran away for fear of the dragon. The dragon arose, adored for two hours, and then returned to his cave, completely cured.

blinded by a stake that had been driven through his eye, was cured by an outstandingly charitable saint.

Quite apart from their ability to wreak destruction directly, dragons were dreaded as omens of catastrophe. The sight of one usually heralded storms, earthquakes, bloodshed and desolation, all of which had been traditionally associated with dragons. Not everybody took these omens with quite the seriousness of a nobleman whose fate was recorded by a fourteenth century scholar. Being told that a dragon had fallen from the sky, and realizing that this was the accepted omen of a prince's death, the nobleman assumed that he was the intended victim, promptly fell ill and died, thereby fulfilling the prophecy. An extreme example of *noblesse oblige*.

It would be unwise and unfair for us to smile too broadly at the credulity of the Middle Ages; time will undoubtedly tell which of our own beliefs and fears were the equivalent of dragons. Besides, we should remember that in the Middle Ages the Church was the undisputed authority, not only in matters of faith but in matters of education and scholarship. It would have been as unwise and unthinkable to doubt the colorful stories by which the

OPPOSITE *So valuable were certain organs of dragons in the practice of alchemy and medicine that men would take extraordinary and sometimes fatal risks to obtain them.*

BELOW *Some exceptional men could handle monsters with impunity. Alexander the Great traveled extensively through the air in a basket drawn by griffins.*

priest supported the dogmas of Christianity as to doubt the dogmas themselves. At a time when life was long in toil and short in pleasure, such diverting and stimulating fables were much appreciated.

Although the dragons of the west were terrifying monsters best avoided, they, like their more benign Chinese cousins, could occasionally serve practical ends.

While there are no eyewitness accounts of dragons being used for transportation, other than in medieval folklore, the belief that this was possible persisted. With the proper magic incantations, dragons could be lured from their lairs, to be saddled and bridled for the journey. Such conviction possibly derived from accounts of the exploits of Alexander the Great, which came mysteriously to light in the Middle Ages and enjoyed a considerable vogue.

The evil that dragons could provoke between human beings did not end in the Garden of Eden.

A Fatal Glance

Wherwell Priory lies in the New Forest area of England. In a dungeon within the Priory lived a cockatrice, hatched by a toad from a duck's egg, and incubated in a dungheap. This unsavory creature was killed by a man named Green by the usual trick of lowering a mirror into the dungeon. The cockatrice, whose very glance was deadly, then caught sight of itself and immediately died.

As classical mythology demonstrated many times, dragons have always harbored a lust for virgins.

Dracontias, a precious gem with mystical powers.

According to these Alexander, whom it will be recalled had a blood tie with dragons, actually preferred griffins for flying. The griffin had wings and four leonine legs with eagles' claws; it differed from the standard dragon only in having an eagle's head, an avian affinity that may have governed Alexander's preference. Sometimes the king went aloft astride a single griffin, but more usually he was shown traveling seated with imperial dignity in a wicker basket, a griffin tethered to each corner by a length of chain. Flight was controlled by a large piece of meat on the point of a sword or spear: for ascent, the meat was raised and the griffins flew up in pursuit of it, dragging the basket with them; for descent, the meat was lowered and the griffins flew down to earth. While modern flight technology may be more elaborate, it is scarcely more foolproof. Alexander, who was apparently no mean hand in the traditional skill of dragon slaying, seems equally to have been ahead of his time; another of his innovations was a magic submarine of glass in which he voyaged to the bottom of the sea.

But with European dragons, too, the usefulness of a living dragon was negligible compared to the uses to which its remains could be put. Like the dragons of India and China, it carried in its head a precious gem called "dracontias." Unfortunately, this had to be removed while the dragon was still alive, since dragons at the point of death would deliberately spoil the gem and destroy its magical properties. It is possible that dragons acquired this unhelpful trick from their enemies, the elephants, who according to medieval belief purposely buried their shed tusks to frustrate ivory collectors. The belief, as Rider Haggard's novel *King Solomon's Mines* confirms, persisted into quite recent times.

Obtaining dracontias then, as can be seen, was no work for amateurs. The preferred method was first to put your dragon to sleep, but this called for skills in the use of herbs, charms, and incantations. A second and somewhat dubious technique was to use drums to stimulate thunder. It will be recalled that more ancient dragons were the cause of thunder; apparently European dragons were so nervous of it that they could be startled into emerging from their lairs. No further instructions are given on how to obtain the dracontias from an alarmed and living dragon.

Obviously the powers of dracontias must have been very great indeed to justify the hazards of obtaining it. But it is difficult to deduce exactly what those mystical or occult powers were. Some authorities claimed that dracontias, like alicorn (unicorn's horn), could be used to detect poison, a facility that might be crucial amidst the intrigues for which medieval courts were notorious. A fuller account of the gem's uses is provided, however, by a knight of the Order of St. John of Jerusalem.

Apparently the Chevalier de Gozano, later Grand Master of the Order, slew a dragon on the island of Rhodes sometime around 1345, somehow managing to extract the dracontias before the monster expired. The stone, which became a family heirloom, was about the size of an olive, strikingly

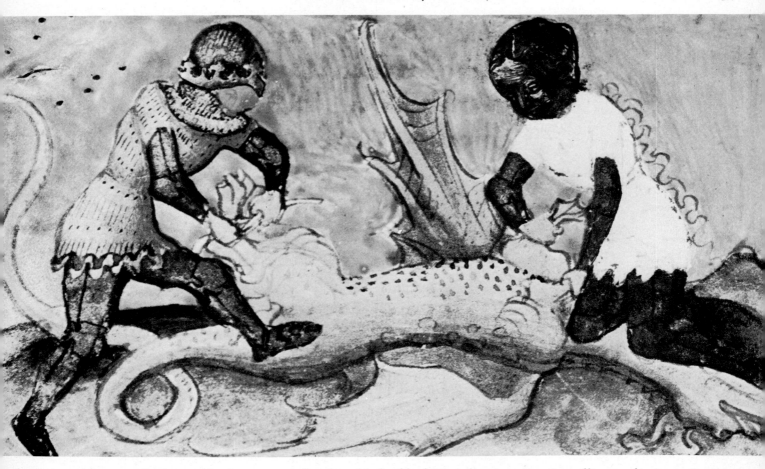

So heavy was the demand for dragons among European alchemists and among Ethiopians, who liked to eat them, that a minor trade war erupted in the thirteenth century.

colored, and indeed had "singular virtue" against all sorts of poisons. It seems that when the gem was put in water, the water boiled and became effective as an antidote. A descendant of de Gozano, Pierre de Gozon-Mélac, who was a Grand Prior of St. Gilles from 1558 to 1561, describes how a man who had drunk the water disgorged a very venomous serpent eighteen inches long. A jaundiced later commentator suggests that the water was merely an emetic and that the "venomous serpent" was a common tapeworm. If this was so, it would seem that obtaining the cure was much more hazardous than the disease.

Almost all other components of a dragon's body, obtainable with far less risk, were invaluable. Not only did they cure many ills of the flesh, but they provided relief from many of the vexations of medieval life:

The dragon's head, buried under a house, will bring good fortune to the

A few medieval notables, a pope among them, did in fact acquire dragons as household pets. Their inordinate daily appetite for human beings must have raised some problems for their owners.

household. Moreover, it "keepeth one from looking asquint."

Dragon fat "dryed in the sunne" was proof against creeping ulcers, in addition to repelling "all venemouse bestes." Mixed with honey and oil, it cured dimness of the eyes; while an amulet made from the fat of a dragon's heart, wrapped in gazelle skin and tied to the upper arm by a deer sinew, ensured victory in lawsuits.

The value of dragon flesh is both specific and obscure. It would seem that the eternal enmity of dragons and elephants derives from the need of dragons to cool themselves by drinking the cold blood of elephants. Consequently, the very cold flesh of dragons is recommended as a food for inhabitants of very hot countries, such as "they of Ethiope."

The tongue, eyes, gall, and intestines when boiled in wine and oil, cooled by nocturnal air, and rubbed on night and morning, dispersed troublesome "night-visions and apparitions." An alternative remedy for the same complaint consisted of dragon's eyes "kept till they be stayle, and afterwards beat into an Oyl with Honey and used as an ointment."

Dragons keep cool with chilled elephant blood.

A Cure for the Stone

For let a man who has within him a kidney or bladder stone take some dragon's blood and put it in a moist place so that it becomes moderately moist; and then let him put this blood into pure and temperate water for a brief time. Meanwhile let him take something hot, and thus having removed the blood, let the fasting man drink moderately from the water, and then eat some food, and let him do so moderately with the blood and water for nine days, and from the strength of the blood, the stone in him will be broken, and so the man will be free of it. No man, however, should eat and drink from the pure and undiluted blood, since if any man does, he will instantly die.

St. Hildegard of Bingen

One of the first concerns of a successful dragon-slayer was to collect the monster's blood, which was much prized for its magical and medicinal properties.

Dragon skin was useful for cooling the passions of lovers, possibly those aroused by the love potions and charms that could be compounded from other parts of dragons.

The first vertebra from a dragon's backbone was considered a useful aid in petitioning those in power, while dragon's teeth wrapped in doeskin and tied on with deer sinew might even make them gracious.

Given the prevalence of dragons, invincibility was much prized in the Middle Ages. That condition was guaranteed by this very popular prescription: An unguent made from the head and tail of a dragon, the marrow of a lion and some hair from its forehead, the paw of a dog, and foam from the mouth of a victorious racehorse. It is probable that the process rather than the product confirmed invincibility.

Of all the by-products of a dragon, the most versatile and efficacious was its blood, which was a staple of medieval medicine and magic. It could cure kidneystones and blindness. It was invaluable to scribes since it would dissolve gold for the illumination of manuscripts; today's chemists, hampered by the acute shortage of dragon's blood, are obliged to use a solution of nitric and hydrochloric acids. Furthermore, when a fire had been started by the sprinkling of hot lion's blood onto one of the Five Magic Stones — a hazard for which few households would be prepared — only dragon's blood was powerful enough to extinguish the flames.

It might be imagined that obtaining a supply of dragon's blood was in itself unduly hazardous, but a thorough knowledge of natural history obviated any risk. When an elephant and a dragon involved themselves in mortal combat, the blood of the dragon eventually soaked into the earth. From that spot a tree would grow, the sap of which would contain dragon's blood, or cinnabar. Other sources of dragon's blood were the "bloodstone" haematite, an ore rich in iron, and mineral cinnabar, a compound of mercury.

Not unnaturally, in the Middle Ages and later, alternative sources of dragons' blood were much sought after. One particular dragon's blood tree achieved widespread fame. It was an enormous specimen of the species that is still called *Dracaena draco* by botanists, and it was discovered and identified

The resin of the dragon's blood tree is useful in embalming.

by European visitors on the island of Tenerife in 1406. Local people then held it to be already very ancient, and worshiped it as their divine protector. They also collected the resin that oozed from it which they used for various purposes, including the embalming of their dead. Despite all the attention it attracted, the tree survived well into the nineteenth century.

Following that discovery, the other dragon's blood trees of the Canary Islands were thoroughly exploited for the European trade, as were similar stands of trees in the East Indies and southern Arabia. Incisions were made in the bark and the sap collected as it congealed into resin. Long after the Middle Ages, it continued to be used as a means of stopping bleeding, as an astringent mouthwash, and as an ingredient in the varnish applied to violins.

Inevitably, the growing demand for dragons and their derivatives led to commercial conflict. In the thirteenth century, Friar Roger Bacon complained that "it is certain" that Ethiopian sages were coming to Europe — to "those Christian lands where there are good flying dragons" — luring dragons from their caves, saddling them, and then riding them back to Ethiopia where the beasts would be butchered and eaten. A century later European merchants, having belatedly grasped the commercial possibilities of the dragon trade, had established their own agents locally to acquire dragons for export to Ethiopia. It can be assumed that they advertised European dragons as a superior breed, and charged accordingly.

125

The profession of alchemy, because the penalties for sorcery were so severe, was almost as hazardous as that of dragon-slaying.

Regrettably, less scrupulous traders began to exploit their more gullible customers with spurious dragons and dragon products. Wise consumers of dragons' blood could protect themselves by means of a simple test: due to the natural antipathy between dragons and eagles, the blood of a dragon would not mix with that of an eagle. And so all that was needed for the test was some authenticated eagles' blood. In time, no doubt, a trade in bogus eagles' blood resulted.

Other dragon products were less easy to authenticate, and it is certain that appropriately-modified skeletons and organs from a variety of creatures reached the market. Many of these are recorded, such as the skeleton of a flying dragon presented, in good faith, to Cardinal Barberini by King Louis XIII of France. With the best of intentions, a seventeenth century consumer advocate revealed how such a false dragon could be fabricated from the carcass of a skate or ray. In all probability he helped perpetuate the practice he was attempting to condemn. Modified fish remains of this kind can still be found in London antique stores.

Modern physics concerns itself with two vast and intractable questions: the fundamental nature of matter and the workings of the universe. Centuries have not much altered these concerns: in the Middle Ages and even earlier, the same two questions also attracted many of the most subtle minds of the day to the related studies of alchemy and astrology. Basically, alchemy was the investigation of the properties of matter and astrology those of the universe. Where modern physicists may talk quite graphically of the curvature of space, of black holes, and of quarks and quasars, medieval alchemists and astrologers seeking the same goals had to be more circumspect and speak in more arcane terms. After all, the Church had decreed that the creation of the universe was simply explained in the Book of Genesis: scholars, who depended for their livelihoods and indeed for their lives on the goodwill of the Church could not dispute that explanation too openly.

While much genuine and practical chemical knowledge was acquired by alchemists, it was merely incidental to their obsessive search for the Philosopher's Stone, the means of transmuting base metals such as copper and lead into gold, or for the elixir that would confer immortality upon mankind.

Full understanding of the hidden nature of things would be entrusted only

So jealously guarded were the secret processes of medieval alchemy that few scientists today know how to fully utilize the organs of dragons and other creatures.

to a select few. Obviously persistence alone was not enough: Thomas Charnock, a sixteenth century alchemist, repeated one experiment 476 times without success. To be a suitable recipient of the hidden knowledge, one had also to be pure, upright, and high-minded. As one authority put it in the fifteenth century, alchemy could only be taught to:

> ... a perfect man to God and also full of chariti
> Doing alle waies good deede and ... full of humilitie.

Alchemy was not just the ineffectual dabbling in primitive chemistry it sometimes seems to us; for the true aspirant it was no less than a sacred quest, where the ostensible search for the transforming Stone symbolized the redemption of sinful man by God's grace. These two threads – practical chemistry on the one hand and mystic theology on the other – wind through the evolution of medieval thought.

Arrival at the goal, the successful transmutation of base metal into gold, was considered a rare achievement. But when it did occur, it could endow the fortunate alchemist with priceless riches, both material and spiritual. For this reason, even the most elementary of processes had to be cloaked in secrecy; there was the danger not only of being robbed, but of being accused of heresy and sorcery. And quite apart from the alchemist's personal safety, there was a need to guard those precious secrets of nature from the eyes of the uninitiated, those who lacked the requisite purity of spirit and who had not, by persistent and singleminded dedication, earned the right to such valuable knowledge. As a consequence, alchemists never described what they were doing in literal and simple terms, but resorted instead to cryptic metaphors and subtle allusions, language understandable only by the initiated. Scientists today, while they may deny any link with alchemists, have perpetuated that cryptic tradition.

From the swirling mists of that professional obscurity, the dragon emerges once again. Some alchemists considered the dragon symbolic of the *prima materia* from which the Philosopher's Stone might be derived. There were at

OPPOSITE *For alchemists, dragons had a symbolic meaning beyond their practical use. Drawings and tapestries that once had a deeper significance are now merely decorative.*

BELOW *According to alchemists, a dragon inspirited could be transformed into a philosopher's tree.*

Dragons also played a symbolic role in
portraying the philosophical concept of
the Conjunction of Opposites.

Certain dragons were notorious for their vast and indiscriminate appetite for lesser species, a fact later overlooked by Charles Darwin in propounding his theories.

least fifty definitions of *prima materia*. Besides being known as "The Dragon," it was identified with iron, lead, silver, salt, sulphur, the moon, chaos, quicksilver, and other elements. Quicksilver, or mercury, associated with the planet of that name, linked the twin sciences of alchemy and astrology, but was also thought to be either the seed or the bile of a dragon. And a dragon with four heads was felt to symbolize the four degrees of fire. When a medieval alchemist wrote that "the dragon never dies, except with his brother and wife and sister," he was not stressing the extent of family

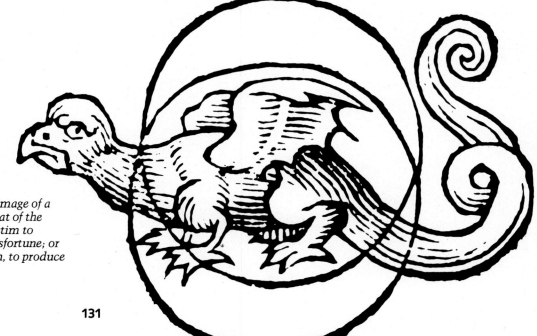

Another occult use of the image of a dragon, combined with that of the moon, was to subject a victim to anguish, infirmity, and misfortune; or in a different conformation, to produce a renewal of youth.

131

Draconem nostrum vivum date devorandum leoni ferocissimo.

Childe Wynd & the Laidly Worm

A long time ago there lived in Bamburgh Castle, Northumbria, a king who had a wife and two children, a son known as Childe Wynd and a daughter called Margaret. Childe Wynd left home to seek his fortune and, soon after, the queen died. The king remarried. His new wife was a witch as well as a queen, for when she became jealous of Margaret's beauty, she turned the girl into a loathsome dragon or Laidly Worm. Margaret was fated to remain in this form:

Until Childe Wynd, the king's own son
Come to the Heugh and thrice kiss thee.

The Laidly Worm crawled out of the castle and took up residence on the nearby crag or Heugh of Spindleston. Driven by hunger, she began to make periodic sorties in search of food, devouring anything that crossed her path. On the advice of a local wise man, these depredations were stopped by supplying her daily with the milk of seven cows. Soon Childe Wynd heard what had happened and set off for home. Despite the storms and men-at-arms raised against him by his stepmother, he managed to land from his ship. He was just about to chop off the head of the dragon when he heard it say in the voice of his sister Margaret: ·

O quit your sword, unbend your bow,
And give me kisses three;
For though I am a poisonous worm,
No harm I'll do to thee.

He bent low over the horrible monster and kissed it three times, whereupon it was immediately transformed back into the shape of his sister. After turning his stepmother into a toad, he ascended his father's throne and ruled as king for many years.

OPPOSITE *Art has recorded the imprisonment of a three-headed dragon in a vast phial, possibly in Augsburg, and the passage overhead of the sun god in his chariot. There is no mention of this incident in history books.*

loyalty within the species but alluding to an obscure alchemical process. Another recurrent image of alchemy, possibly borrowed from ancient mythology, was that of the dragon biting its own tail, referred to as the Uroboros, which is Greek for "tail-biter." In biting its tail, the Uroboros was believed to be simultaneously consuming, fertilizing, and giving birth to itself: symbolizing the cycle of death, fertilization, and birth in a single image. The symbolism apparently encompassed the process of alchemy, which begins and ends with the One, *prima materia*.

Astrology, the science that equaled alchemy in importance during the Middle Ages, was concerned with the hidden meanings and patterns of the universe rather than with the qualities of physical elements. It is similar, however, in its cryptic obscurity, from which the dragon again rears its meaningful head. Observation of the constellation Draco, the Dragon, formed when the monster Ladon, in compensation for his defeat by Herakles, was given a place in the heavens, was said to be of great practical value. When the "head" of the Dragon occupied certain positions in the sky, one's wishes might be granted.

The image of a dragon biting its tail was called the Uroboros, Greek for "tail-biter," which symbolized the cycle of death, fertilization, and birth. In the terms of alchemy, the One, prima materia, *leads back to the One.*

Pope Gregory's stylish slaying of a dragon, with the adept assistance of an aide, Leandro, seems to have been omitted from papal histories.

Although the tradition of obscurity established by both alchemy and astrology has been preserved, the practice of alchemy faded with the waning of the Middle Ages and was replaced by more systematic physical sciences; as we can tell from our morning newspapers, however, astrology is still widely practiced, without having improved its methods in the slightest since the Middle Ages. To be fair, alchemy did bequeath us a little genuine technical knowledge, and both sciences did greatly enrich literature, legend, and folklore with their picturesque if baffling imagery. But the dragon owes them the greater debt, since they helped to etch its image even more vividly in the popular imagination.

Quite apart from the general run of dragon lore which offered a fanciful jumble of information about the monsters, their habits, their physical characteristics, and their uses, medieval legend is rich in tales of encounters with specific individual dragons. Almost invariably these follow the ancient trad-

ition of god or hero triumphing over a fierce and hideous monster, although in keeping with the times the god or hero is replaced by a saint or by a king or knight of impeccable character and immaculate virtue.

The familiar paragon of dragon-slayers is, of course, St. George. "St. George and the Dragon" conjures up an immediate picture of the knight in shining armor on his rearing steed transfixing his awful adversary with a lance. The history of St. George is in reality, if that word is appropriate, a great deal richer and more fascinating than that simple image suggests.

In the first place, the identity – and even the existence – of the saint is in doubt, to say nothing of his saintliness. Two early accounts offer sharply contrasting beginnings to his history. About A.D. 315, Eusebius, who was Bishop of Caesaria in Asia Minor, wrote of a man who had been martyred a dozen years before for tearing down the Emperor Diocletian's decree against

St. George then looking round about,
The fiery dragon soon espy'd,
And like a knight of courage stout,
Against him did most fiercely ride;
And with such blows he did him greet,
He fell beneath his horse's feet.

For with his launce that was so strong,
As he came gaping in his face,
In at his mouth he thrust along;
For he could pierce no other place:
And thus within the lady's view
This mighty dragon straight he slew.

The savour of his poisoned breath
Could do this holy knight no harm.
Thus he the lady sav'd from death,
And home he led her by the arm;
Which when king Ptolemy did see,
There was great mirth and melody.

RIGHT *Despite the competition of mortals, the Archangel Michael has remained the celestial bane of dragons.*

OPPOSITE *St. George, whose popularity may be owed to a military reputation, was the doyen of dragon-slayers, and the idol of muscular Christians.*

BELOW *While St. George may have lacked the subtlety of other saintly dragon-slayers, he lent panache and dramatic appeal to the profession.*

Christians. This occurred in the town of Nicomedia, capital of the Roman province of Bithynia. Eusebius does not mention the name of the martyr and adds only that he was "of no mean origin." Nevertheless, a common belief developed that his name had been George, that he had been born (and buried) in Lydda, between Jerusalem and Jaffa, that he had grown up in Cappadocia in eastern Turkey, and that he had once served in the Roman army.

*St. George's fame transcended time and space. He was as celebrated in Ethiopia (*BELOW*) as in medieval Germany (*OPPOSITE*), and pictorially adopted by each culture.*

The alternative George, if he was not better than he should have been, is better documented. He, too, had a connection with the Roman army, but as a dishonest supplier of provisions in Constantinople. When his fraud was discovered, he evaded justice by fleeing to Cappadocia, crossing legendary paths with the other George. Eventually, he emerged from the acrid politics and theological controversies of the early Church as Bishop of Alexandria, only to die at the hands of a mob there.

Whichever is the real St. George, and the shadowy martyr of Nicomedia

RIGHT AND BELOW *If art is to be believed, dragons during St. George's extended lifetime must have become an endangered species. The range of his deadly operations was astounding.*

seems the preferable candidate, a popular and widespread cult furthered his legend. This popularity may be attributable to his military background. While many new Christians may have seen service with the Roman army, there were few soldier-saints to identify with. Although the cult of St. George continued to spread gradually throughout Europe, it was not until the Middle

Ages that it regained its early popularity. Apparently the soldiers who took part in the Crusade felt an affinity with St. George; if accounts of their barbarous behavior are to be believed, Crusaders were also in need of a saint to intercede for them on Judgment Day.

Few Christian saints have generated as many conflicting myths as St. George, and few have been martyred as frequently and as gruesomely as he was: he is described variously as having been crushed to death, made to run in red-hot iron boots, scourged, cast into a well with a heavy stone tied round his neck, beaten with sledgehammers, roasted, poisoned, and buried alive in quicklime. Yet after every episode he was restored miraculously to life and

The hazardous road to sainthood was paved with slain dragons.

Distress caused by dragons among damsels seems to have been a major social problem throughout the Middle Ages and the Renaissance.

health. In between martyrdoms, this incorrigible survivor performed several miracles and converted 40,900 souls to the Faith. Amongst his final conversions was the Empress of Persia, but this so enraged her husband, the Emperoror, that he had St. George decapitated forthwith and permanently. The date of this ultimate martyrdom was April 23, which is still commemorated as St. George's Day.

It may have been noticed that no dragon has made an appearance in these early accounts of St. George's very active life. This omission was not remedied until almost a thousand years after the saint's last death, when Jacques de Voragine wrote his *Legenda Aurea*, or "Golden Legend," in the thirteenth century. De Voragine tells of the city of Silene in Libya which was menaced by a dragon in a nearby lake with breath so foul that it poisoned the countryside. To keep the monster at bay, it had been necessary to provide a daily

RIGHT AND OPPOSITE *St. George's feats commanded the attention of artists throughout the civilized world and continued to do so until quite recent times.*

sacrifice of two sheep. But eventually, when the supply of sheep ran out, human substitutes had to be offered. An ordinance required that children should be chosen by lot to be fed to the dragon and, eventually, the king's daughter was selected and was led out to be sacrificed.

At this moment St. George, in the role of knight errant, makes a timely appearance. He asks the princess what is happening; she tells him, and beseeches him to save himself by fleeing. Naturally, St. George stands his

ground and, when the dragon emerges from the lake, smites it with his spear, "and hurt him sore." The dragon is so seriously wounded (and possibly so astonished) that it is led meekly back into the city by the princess. St. George makes a brief oration, baptizes the entire population and then, with a striking want of Christian forgiveness, lops off the dragon's head.

Later versions allow a little more embroidery. A printed account in verse dating from 1515 makes George "the captayne of certayne legion of men of armys"; the "great and foul dragon" is more awesomely described, and the princess, whose proffered hand in marriage the saint courteously declines, is given the name Alcyone.

In 1349, King Edward III made St. George the patron saint of England (displacing the previous incumbent, Edward the Confessor); a curious choice, given the English love of all animals other than foxes and game birds.

OPPOSITE, ABOVE, AND RIGHT *In 1349 St. George was made the patron saint of England. Within a couple of centuries his Middle Eastern origin was forgotten and he was considered an Englishman, born in Coventry. An attempt by Pope Clement VII to disassociate St. George from dragons was in vain.*

The recent decanonization of St. George by the Vatican has not diminished the loyalty of the English to their lethal patron saint.

But the following year, George was further honored as patron of the newly created Order of the Garter. St. George's Chapel in Windsor Castle, where the ceremonies of the Order are held to this day, later acquired "the herte of Saynte George: which Sygysmond the Emperor of Alamayn brought and gaf it for a grete and precyous relique to kynge Harry the fifte. And also there is a piece of his head." Apparently other heads of St. George lay in Rome and in the church of Mares-Moutier in Picardy; his arms were kept as relics in Cambrai, Toulouse, and Cologne; and various other organs were liberally installed elsewhere. Not merely a great saint, but a man of many parts.

In the early sixteenth century, after a tenure of less than three hundred years, the dragon was dismissed from official accounts of St. George's life by

Pope Clement VII. Possibly to express disdain for Rome, the English retained the dragon in their legends. An eighteenth century version accorded St. George, a Levantine saint of some fifteen hundred years' standing, English citizenship. His birthplace became Coventry rather than Lydda. His father is identified as "Lord Albert." As the legend goes, George's mother died giving

RIGHT AND ABOVE *Devotees of St. George praise his classical approach to dragon-slaying, the single-handed combat between hero and monster. They disdain the use of such trickery as has immobilized this Nordic dragon, or the Archangel Michael's deployment of heavenly hosts to defeat a dragon.*

RIGHT AND BELOW *By all artistic accounts, the Archangel Michael was in fact a classicist in dragon-slaying and rarely needed to call for outside help.*

St. George finally succumbs to a particularly venomous dragon.

birth to him, and the infant was kidnapped by an enchantress named Kalyb, a loss that struck Lord Albert dead with grief. Kalyb brought George up, and gave him a present of a suit of impregnable armor. In this, George set off for Egypt where, not unexpectedly, the whole country was terrorized by a dragon. This dragon, obviously conventional in its tastes, had been devouring a virgin a day and, inevitably, supplies were down to the king's daughter, whose turn coincided nicely with George's arrival. He slew the dragon and on this occasion, after a number of tribulations, did marry the princess, whose name was Sabra. Having survived a dragon, Sabra eventually succumbed to a horse, dying in a riding accident many years later. Stricken with grief, George made a pilgrimage to the Holy Land, which must have seemed vaguely familiar. But on his return to England, he encountered a second dragon at a place called Dunsmore Heath. While he did slay it with his customary efficiency, he was splattered with its poison during the encounter and died in bed two days later. This ending may seem to bear a striking resemblance to the legendary death of England's own Beowulf. The adaptation is forgivable since familiarity adds credibility; the chequered history of St. George had always been short on credibility.

ABOVE AND RIGHT *Even when preoccupied with weighing the souls of the dead, the Archangel Michael seemed capable of dispatching dragons with rare panache. He appears to be as adept with the sword as with the lance.*

Despite all the celebrity he attracted, St. George was just one of a host of dragon-slaying saints, and one of the duller, more conservative ones at that. Like St. Theodore and the Archangel Michael, he was a muscular Christian who depended largely on brawn and military skill in his slaughter of dragons. The many saints who repulsed monsters by power of faith alone display far greater ingenuity and finesse. And since dragons had long symbolized evil incarnate, and eventually were used to portray such specific evils as paganism, or heresy, or some of the seven deadly sins, faith was obviously a more appropriate weapon than the sword. Unfortunately such spiritual concepts are difficult to portray in painting or sculpture, and most simple churchgoers took the artistic portrayals of confrontations between saints and symbolic dragons quite literally. Similarly, the metaphorical excesses of preachers in the same vein were often taken as gospel truth. At least they concentrated the minds of worshipers most wonderfully.

One such flamboyant example of evil overcome deals with the defeat of the Tarasque by St. Martha of Bethany, patron of cooks and housewives. The Tarasque was a dragon that lived on the banks of the Rhône, near the small town of Tarascon. It was larger than an ox, with a lion's head and teeth, six paws like those of a bear, and a hard skin covered with spikes, ending in a tail of a viper. The Tarasque was the offspring of the ageless and prolific Leviathan and a Bonnacon. The Bonnacon was one of the more unsavory monsters of the medieval bestiaries. Despite the possession of bison-like horns, it defended itself by other means. When evading hunters, it would void the entire contents of its bowel in the face of its pursuers. The excrement, fouling as much as three acres, was so potent that any tree splashed by it burst into flames.

Although it did cause periodic flooding of the Rhône, the Tarasque did not employ the nauseating tactics of its mother. It would emerge from its lair every so often and devour people in the normal way. One day, while it was actually in the process of ingesting a man, St. Martha approached and sprinkled it with holy water, rendering the monster completely tame and

The massive Tarasque is humbled with holy water.

Female saints did not lag behind in dealing with dragons. St. Margaret of Antioch, having repulsed the amorous advances of the local ruler, was cast into a dungeon with a dragon, which she subdued with a crucifix.

An alternative version of the St. Margaret legend recounts that she was actually swallowed by a dragon, which she caused to burst asunder by making the sign of the Cross. Inappropriately, St. Margaret is the patron saint of childbirth, and her emblem is a dragon.

biddable. Unhappily, the local people, who lacked the saint's faith, soon put the harmless Tarasque to death. Until recently, the huge head of a fossilized reptile, exhibited in the nearby city of Aix-en-Provence, was claimed to be that of the Tarasque. The saintly incident is commemorated annually at Whitsun, when an effigy of the monster, spitting fire, is paraded through the town.

The ancient and classical association of dragons with water persisted into the Middle Ages. In Italy, St. Donatus visited a poisoned spring near Arezzo. While he was praying there, a dreadful dragon rose out of the water and coiled its tail round the legs of the saint's donkey. Donatus, abandoning saintly decorum, spat into the monster's mouth; it immediately died and the waters of the spring became wholesome again.

Pope St. Sylvester I displayed more finesse than Donatus in disposing of a fierce dragon that lived in a moat and ate at least three hundred men a day. Sylvester merely uttered the name of Christ and bound up the dragon's jaws with a cord, which he then sealed with the sign of the Cross. His action may have atoned somewhat for that other pontiff reputed to have fed six thousand people a day to his pet dragon. Sylvester is generally represented in religious art leading a small dragon on a chain, so perhaps he, too, took a fancy to the monster.

As can be seen, St. George's drastic methods were probably unnecessary: faith alone, the uttering of Christ's name, or the sign of the Cross were sufficient in most cases. Dragons could even be induced to destroy themselves by such means. St. Hilarion, Archbishop of Palestine, found that the people of Dalmatia were being threatened by a dragon. He ordered them to build a fire and, when it was burning vigorously, commanded the dragon to throw itself onto the flames; the dragon dutifully obeyed and was promptly incinerated.

The moral purpose of medieval legends is evident in the story of St. Margaret of Antioch, whose confrontation with a dragon involved satanic temptation. Osybius, the governor of Antioch, was so captivated by Margaret's beauty that he wished to marry her. She scornfully rejected his proposal and was thrown into a deep dungeon to reconsider her decision. The devil in the

King Arthur was not always as adept in his handling of dragons as this German embroidered picture suggests.

form of a horrible dragon appeared and tried to frighten her from her chosen path of virtue. According to one version of the legend, she merely held up her crucifix and the dragon fled in terror. In another, she was actually swallowed by the monster. With great presence of mind, she made the sign of the Cross and the dragon burst asunder, releasing her. The subsequent choice of St. Margaret as the patron saint of women in childbirth might seem to be rather insensitive.

Since subduing or killing a dragon seemed a guarantee of sainthood, it was a much sought after experience amongst dedicated Christians, whose zeal was rarely diminished by the thought that it might end in martyrdom. The venerable traveler Rufinus, for example, was crossing a North African desert guided by a monk when the party chanced on the tracks of a dragon in the sand. He and his companions were in favor of proceeding on their way, leaving the dragon unmolested, but the monk would not hear of it. He was

Other Arthurian knights had variously rewarding encounters with dragons. Lancelot, (ABOVE) was unwittingly rewarded with a son, Galahad. And Percival (BELOW) safely encountered a dragon in an allegorical vision.

"carried away by impatience and delight at the prospect of this encounter and the opportunity to demonstrate the power of the faith." Rufinus and the others, though willing to take this on trust, were obliged by their enthusiastic guide to follow him as he tracked the dragon to its den. Here, "having taken up a position at the entrance to the beast's lair, he waited for us so as to kill the creature in our presence, and refused to leave until eventually the dragon emerged to be slain." Rufinus adds that a more agreeable companion might have been a certain Nisterion, who went out of his way to avoid meeting a dragon, "not for fear of the animal but on the contrary, to avoid the demon of vanity and the temptation to destroy the animal."

Saints, or would-be saints, did not hold a monopoly over the slaying of dragons. Many monarchs and knights in medieval as in classical times greatly enhanced their heroic prestige by disposing of some fire-spitting monster or other. That paragon of knightly virtue, King Arthur, enjoyed at least one protracted struggle with a dragon. It took place in Britanny near the present-day village of Plestin-les-Grèves. It is not made clear how the encounter began, but after some time Arthur had not prevailed and was on the verge of exhaustion. Fortunately, the king's cousin St. Efflam arrived and, Moses-like, struck the ground with his staff to produce a spring of water, enabling Arthur to refresh himself. The dragon had meanwhile retired to its lair, possibly as exhausted as the king. The saint ordered it to come forth and cast itself into the sea, which it did, with no great credit to the king.

One of King Arthur's knights, however, displayed more fortitude, and in more ways than one. In the medieval romance of the Knights of the Round

The practice of alchemy continued into the seventeenth century and this traditional representation of the dragon symbolizes the properties of mercury.

Table it is related "how syr Launcelot rode on his adventure, and how he helpe a dolorous lady fro hyr payne, and how that he faught wyth a dragon." The dragon in question lay beneath a slab-like tombstone: "soo whan sir Launcelotte had lyffte up the tomb there came oute an orryble and fyendeley dragon spyttyng wilde fyre oute of hys mouthe. Than sir Launcelotte drew his sworde and faught wyth that dragon longe, and at the laste wyth grete payne sir Launcelotte slew that dragon." Being less than saintly, he then proceeded to sleep with the "dolorous lady," whose name was Elaine. Since he had had a lot to drink, Launcelot was under the impression at the time that his companion was Guinevere, his queen and Arthur's wife. Unseemly though it may have been, the episode did result in the birth of Galahad, the most perfect and chivalrous of all of Arthur's knights.

Another redoubtable dragon-slayer was Deodatus de Gozano, the knight of the Order of St. John who was to bequeath his family a dracontias stone. The dragon that Deodatus put paid to lived on the island of Rhodes, a resort of many reptiles, and seems to have been an impressive specimen. It was about the size of a horse and had the head and neck of a serpent, with long ears like those of a mule but covered in scales. Its four legs resembled those of a crocodile and ended in bear-like claws; its wings were black or perhaps blue above, and yellow and green or red below; and the monster's tail was so long that it coiled several times around the body. When it charged, it beat its wings, fire flashed from its eyes, and a terrible hissing rent the air.

The dragon's lair was in a cavern in the valley of Soudourli, at the foot of Mount St. Stephen. From this it would sally forth every so often, polluting the air with its poisonous breath and killing any men or animals in the vicinity. So ferocious was it that even the valiant knights of the Order who ruled the island at the time were forbidden to hazard their lives by approaching the place, on pain of expulsion from the Order.

Deodatus, on the assumption that valor was the better part of discretion, decided to disobey and rid the island of its affliction. Having studied the situation, he withdrew to Provence. There he constructed a model of the dragon which could be made to thrash around and beat its wings in a realistic manner by servants pulling on cords. Using this, he accustomed his charger and two English bulldogs to the sight of the dragon and trained the dogs to attack it without hesitation.

On his return to Rhodes, Deodatus first offered up prayers in the church of St. Stephen and then set out for the dragon's lair. His servants were stationed nearby with instructions to help him if need be, or to run away if they saw him perish. He then rode forward, his lance at the ready. The dragon came rushing out. Deodatus struck it in the shoulder, but the lance splintered on the tough scales. He would have died then and there but for the efforts of his

The Nature of the Dragon

The Dragon is the grettest of all serpentes and bestes, as Ysidor sayth in Inde and in Ethiope be many, & he groweth tyll he be ccvi cubites of lengthe & more, and when he is come to his ful age or strength than lyveth he longe with out mete, but whan he beginneth to ete he is nat lightely suffysed. The dragon dwelleth in depe caves of the grounde, and when he feleth any reyne commynge out of the ayre than commeth he out of his cave or denne & fleeth in to the ayre & bethet in the ayre in suche wyse that it semeth to be a gret tempest in the ayre & his wynges be of a great quantyte accordynge to his body & they be facyoned lyke the winges of a batte that flyeth in the twy lyght & where as the dragon abideth there is the ayre darke & full of venymous corruption.

The Noble Lyfe & Natures of Man, Bestes, Serpentys, Fowles & Fisshes

two dogs, which seized the dragon by the belly as they had been trained to do. This gave the knight time to draw his sword and pierce the dragon's throat, where the skin was less hard. The monster fell dead to the ground, taking Deodatus down with it. But the knight was not dead and, having been revived by his servants, was able to ride slowly and painfully back to the town.

He at once reported his deed to the Grand Master of his Order, who praised his courage but nevertheless expelled him from the Order and threw him in prison for disobedience. After a few days, however, the hero was released and reinstated. Within a few years he was himself Grand Master. When he died in 1353 his tomb was inscribed with the words "Draconis Exstinctor," meaning "Exterminator of the Dragon."

An alternative version of the slaying of the dragon of Rhodes, less flattering to the valorous knight, circulated among local Muslims. According to them, the slayer sought the help of a dervish, or holy man. On the dervish's advice, he collected forty asses and loaded them with sacks of quicklime. When these were led to the mouth of the cavern, the dragon came leaping out and devoured both the animals and their loads. It then washed the meal down by drinking from a nearby river. Water added to quicklime generates extreme heat of course, and the dragon perished in great agony.

This unorthodox method of slaying a dragon is familiar. It will be remembered from the Book of Bel that in Babylon Daniel used a similar inflammable meal to detonate a dragon. And King Cracus of Poland, founder of Krakow, also adopted this stratagem: "There was a Dragon which lived on a rock, and which when compelled to do so from hunger, used to creep from its cave and kill many people. Three oxen were daily brought to the cave of this monster. The King of the country, moved with compassion for his people, ordered at last

Dragons had been adopted as important symbols in heraldry. In this section of the Bayeux tapestry, showing the Battle of Hastings, dragons are for once aloof from the bloodshed.

a calf's skin be filled with pitch, sulphur and nitre, and offered to the beast. The Dragon was deceived by this trick, and with one bellow from its vitals perished on the spot."

Other legends of this internal combustion of dragons are part of the lore of places far removed from Rhodes or Babylon. The combustible materials tend to reflect local circumstances; in the Scottish Borders and on the Shetland Isles, peat was the unlikely fuel used. But in its essentials the legend is so invariably the same no matter where it is recounted that it must stem from some common, and probably ancient, source. One of the likelier sources would be the apocryphal Book of Bel and the Dragon which, despite its omission from the authorized Testaments, would be known within the Church by scholars and priests; and of course the Church surpassed even merchants as a disseminator of ideas in the Middle Ages. But whoever spread that particular basic legend, it is worth reflecting that for simple and relatively powerless people the idea of outwitting a dragon was probably more appealing than that of destroying it by force of arms. And it put dragon-slaying within the means of humble local heroes.

Because dragon-slaying was, for the most part, a noble profession, dragons were accorded a place in the realm of heraldry. The function of heraldry in the Middle Ages was to identify a person who would otherwise be anonymous with his armor, and to overawe his opponents with a display of martial splendor. Inevitably a colorful variety of dragons found their way onto knightly coats of arms, crests and banners, and many of them can be found there still.

Obviously the symbolic use of dragons is ancient and is not confined to medieval nobility. For instance, the god Marduk was often depicted with a

The French monarch, François I, adopted as his heraldic device the salamander, a sort of dragon that could live amidst flames and that was so cold by nature that it could extinguish the flames by touching them. The king's somewhat chilling motto, Nutrisco et extinguo, *means "I nourish and extinguish."*

Despite the ignominious fate of so many dragons at the hands of St. George, England's rulers frequently included them in their coats-of-arms as a symbol of indomitable power. Henry VI's arms (ABOVE RIGHT) are a striking example but totally misrepresent the weakness and misery of England under his rule.

dragon at his feet; while it is true that Marduk dismembered Tiamat when he had slain her, the presence of a dragon instantly identifies him. In the same way, a female medieval saint, carrying cooking pot and spoon and with a dragon at her feet, can only be St. Martha of Bethany, patron saint of cooks and housewives and tamer of the Tarasque; artistic license allows the bull-sized dragon to be suitably scaled down.

The use of a dragon to intimidate enemies is often mentioned by classical writers. The army of the later Roman Empire used a *draco* as the standard of a cohort, roughly 500 men, while an eagle standard signified the larger formation of a legion. The *draco* was a windsock in the shape of a flying dragon, and may well have helped archers to gauge wind direction as well as sowing terror in the ranks of the enemy. The Romans had adopted it from a number of tribes in the eastern Empire, such as the Parthians and the Dacians.

The psychological impact of such standards can be judged from an account of clashes with the Parthians. Here, the Roman historian Lucian derides the fearful credulity of an earlier observer:

For all his professed distaste for noble pomp, Oliver Cromwell's coat-of-arms, complete with dragon, is no less grandiose than those of his royal predecessors. Many of his subjects, particularly in Ireland, might have preferred to be ruled by an actual dragon.

Dragons find peace on noble coats-of-arms.

... he has seen everything so keenly that he said that the serpent of the Parthians (this is a banner they use to indicate number — a serpent precedes, I think, a thousand men), he said they were alive and of enormous size; that they were born in Persia a little way beyond Iberia; that they are bound to long poles and, raised on high, create terror while the Parthians are coming on from a distance; that in the encounter itself at close quarters they are freed and sent against the enemy; that in fact they had swallowed many of our men and coiled themselves around others and suffocated and crushed them ...

Little wonder that dragons established a reality when they could be witnessed taking part in human battles.

When the Roman legions left Britain their dragons remained. What was unmistakably a *draco* is shown flying above the head of the ill-fated Harold at the battle of Hastings; possibly he was seeking inspiration from it when he met his downfall. And even later in English history, there are references to dragon standards. Some of these later standards were made more fearsome by the incorporation of combustible materials. The Arthurian magician may even have been the inventor: "... Merlin turned the dragon in his hand and it threw out flames from its mouth so that the air all became reddened ..."

Several kings of England used the dragon on conventional banners and many used dragons as supporters to their arms — that is, as the figures that appear to be propping up the shield on either side. Only with the union of the Scottish and English thrones in 1603 was the dragon permanently deposed as supporter in favor of the lion.

This griffin is from the arms of Gray's Inn, one of the English Inns of Court. Anyone who has ever challenged the law must consider it an appropriate symbol.

Medieval heraldry was a very exacting art with strict rules governing the depiction of heraldic motifs, restrictions on who was entitled to display them, and dire retribution awaiting those who claimed arms to which they were not entitled. Much depended on how a dragon was depicted: whether it was rampant (two forelegs raised), passant (one foreleg raised), or statant (all four feet on the ground); whether its wings were endorsed (upright over the back), displayed or depressed; whether its tail was nowed (knotted); and, of course, whether the color was or, gules, sable, or vert (gold, red, black, or green).

Distinctions were also drawn between the varieties of dragon. Heraldry could not countenance the vague descriptions applied to legendary dragons. A heraldic dragon had four legs and two wings. A dragon with two legs is correctly termed a wyvern; when "blazoned proper" it must have a green head, back, and legs; its chest, belly, and the insides of its wings must be red. A dragon or wyvern lacking wings ("sans wings") is technically a lindworm, a serpent with wings but without legs is an amphiptère, and a serpent or dragon lacking wings and legs is a guivre. The many-headed Hydra and other mythical monsters also make occasional appearances.

It is strange surely that the dragon, a symbol of evil, came to be proudly borne in heraldry by so many noble families. In some cases it represents a heraldic pun on the name of the bearer: the families of de Drago, von Drachenfels, de Draek, de Dragon de Ramillies, and Dragomanni all carry a dragon on the coat of arms, and the family of Sir Francis Drake bore "argent, a wyvern, wings endorsed gules." Sometimes it is used to commemorate an ancestor who is supposed to have slain a dragon, but in many cases it is probable that the legend was created to support the emblem.

The symbolic implications sought, of course, were not the moral ones of sin and evil, but the flattering ones of strength, fierceness, and invincibility, qualities that any noble family would be glad to claim.

But surely it is even stranger that the dragon should have survived the scrutiny of the Renaissance and the skepticism of the Age of Reason, and should still enjoy a menacing, symbolic place in our lives.

Amidst the chaos preceding the Day of
Judgment, the dragons who have so
long supported crowns in heraldry will
be wearing them.

n Europe the Renaissance reawakened the cultural energy and spirit of inquiry that had made the classical eras of Greece and Rome exciting times to live in. While they acknowledged the classical heritage of art, literature, and thought, the men of the Renaissance felt entitled to question it, to explore beyond it, and to compose their own picture of the world. In the light of this scrutiny and skepticism, many medieval notions and superstitions and dogmas were challenged and discarded. Alchemy, for example, was largely displaced by genuine fledgling sciences, and astrology was superseded by astronomy. Strangely enough, the dragon not only survived this scrutiny but achieved a renewed reality: it emerged from the shadows of hearsay and legend and was accepted as an authentic creature in the animal world.

What revolutionized literature and science was the invention of the printed book. Before printing arrived written information had been so laborious and expensive to produce that it had been available only to a privileged few; knowledge was disseminated to men in general only by word of mouth. What ordinary men knew about the world tended to be vague and inaccurate and, because the Church largely controlled written sources of knowledge, to be highly selective.

At first, the early printers devoted their craft simply to reproducing existing manuscript works that had already proved their popularity, giving a new lease on life to old myths and fables. But before long, printing had generated a new breed of literature, nourished by the Renaissance spirit of inquiry and exploration. A number of treatises on animals appeared that differed significantly from the quaint bestiaries assembled in the Middle Ages. One of

PREVIOUS PAGE *While the invention of the printing press encouraged men to free their minds from the limitations of medieval thought, art and imagery still reflected the heritage of ancient myth and fable.*

the most successful of these new books, typical of the change in attitude, is the *Historia Animalium* of Conrad Gesner. Published between 1551 and 1558, with another volume appearing in 1587 after Gesner's death, it amounted to an astonishing 3500 pages, and soon ran to several editions and translations.

Of the translations, one of the most popular was the partial translation into English by Edward Topsell. Topsell's first book, drawn from Gesner's original, appeared in 1607 under the title *The History of Foure-Footed Beastes. Describing the true and lively figure of every Beast, with a discourse of their severall Names, Conditions of their breed, their love and hate to Mankinde, and the wonderfull worke of God in their Creation* ... The following year, encouraged by the success of his initial venture, Topsell added his translation of Gesner's volume on serpents and allied beasts.

Gesner was very much a Renaissance man. Unlike almost all of his medieval predecessors, he was interested in zoology – in animals as animals, not merely bearers of moral significance. An innovation that derives from this approach is his effort to apply some scientific method to his study. Not only does he try to include every animal known to mankind, but he arranges the entries systematically in alphabetical order. Most are illustrated by woodcuts so accurate that the animals are still easily recognizable.

Within each entry the information is arranged in a uniform pattern. First, a "discourse of their severall Names" and the derivation of those names; this followed by a summary of what the great classical authorities say about the species in question; then some more recent information is given. By modern

For long the subject of art and accepted heraldic symbols (ABOVE), dragons now became the focus of a growing scientific curiosity (RIGHT).

The fact that dragons became the subject of learned treatises and bestiaries did not deter artists such as Breughel from using them as subjects of fantasy.

RIGHT AND BELOW *The natural philosophers of the Renaissance, despite the haphazard nature of the evidence, categorized, described, and graphically depicted the various kinds of dragons. Even extraordinarily convincing fake dragons, fashioned from fish such as skates and rays, attracted enormous interest.*

standards this may seem rudimentary as a "scientific" approach, but Gesner does not repeat the information uncritically as a medieval scholar might have done. He feels the need to question curious and unbelievable facts, and often pits one authority against another in an attempt to arrive at the truth.

Under such probing examination, many of the more bizarre creatures of the earlier bestiaries are exposed as figments of imagination. But others begin to

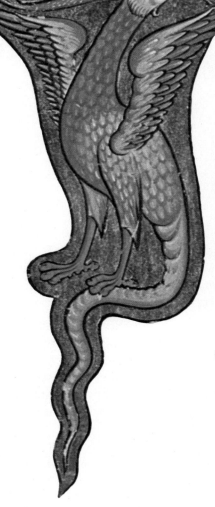

Dragon Supreme

... our description of the Dragon included the right of dominion (so to speak) which it wields over other reptiles. Thus, from its incontrovertible supremacy, writers have given it the name of "king." Although the basilisk must not be cheated out of its name and dignity, yet it must only be taken into consideration when speaking of the smaller reptiles. The Dragon is the largest, bravest, most powerful, and most formidable of all reptiles. These are all royal prerogatives ... Its

strength lies in its tail, and it can use it to such good effect that elephants of great bulk fall before it. In the same way the elephant itself fights with its trunk, the lion with its claws, the horse with its hoof, the ox with its horns, the boar with its flashing tusk, and the wolf with its teeth. No power can avail to release anything once folded within the embrace of its enveloping coils. If small snakes and ordinary Serpents can break a man's arm, what must we think of the power of the Dragon?

George Caspard Kirchmayer

With illustrations as exacting in detail as these, it was little wonder that reported sightings of dragons were more frequent than ever and were no longer confined to knightly heroes and saints.

appear more real and are stripped of their less credible characteristics. The dragon is one of these: not only does it persist but it seems more plausible than ever before. In Topsell's edition, the entry on dragons runs to no fewer than fifteen pages; according to Topsell, "Among all kindes of Serpents, there is none comparable to the Dragon."

Most of the classical references found in Topsell's translation are familiar. We are told of the Roman *draco*; of the golden apples of the Hesperides, guarded by a ferocious dragon; of the flying serpents of Arabia and the two sorts of dragons in India; of how guile must be used to obtain the magical gems possessed by dragons; of the virtues of other portions of the dragon's anatomy; of the methods used by heroes in slaying dragons, and of the herbs by which dragons cure their illnesses; and, naturally, of the eternal enmity between dragons and elephants. Gesner and many of his contemporaries held fast to the traditional belief in natural antipathies between certain animals. And so, even in the seventeenth century, naturalists were still puzzled by the unreasoning hostility between elephants and dragons. After that time, when the Age of Reason had succeeded the Renaissance, there are no further reports of this struggle; presumably these two very intelligent beasts decided there were no reasonable grounds for continuing it.

Italian Ulisse Aldrovandus attempted in his lifetime to catalogue everything in the natural world. Only three volumes were published before he died at 83. Serpents and dragons comprised Volume X.

OPPOSITE *Dragons have always been particularly partial to virgins.*

It must be conceded that the skepticism of the Renaissance man was not limitless. "I will not mingle fables and truth together," affirms Topsell; he then proceeds to recount how a dragon fell in love with a youth in Thessaly. Again, religious values supersede zoological ones when he considers a Roman story of a dragon in a sacred grove "unto the which Dragon the Virgins came every year being blinde-folded with clowts, and carrying Marchpanes in their hands … and so every one of the Virgins did severally offer up their Marchpanes to the Dragon: the Dragon received the Marchpane at the hand of every pure Virgin and unspotted, but if they were defiled, and held only the name of Virgins, then the Dragon refused the Marchpane, and therefore they were all examined at their coming forth, and those which had lost their Virginity might be punished by the Law." The Reverend Topsell's attitude is unyielding: this story "none but Heathens will believe to be true, because it is a fable merely invented to defend Idolatry, which with my soul and spirit I do detest." Fortunately, there are stories involving Christian maidens that can be substituted to enhance the credibility of dragons.

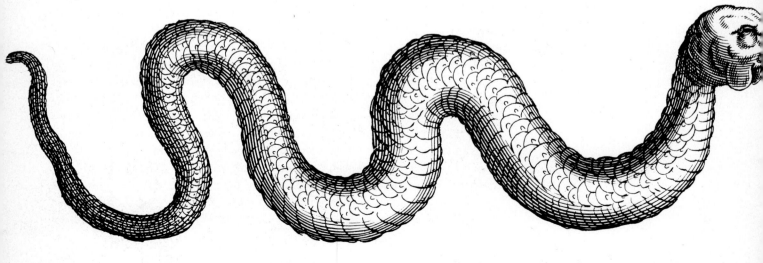

Mortal Coils

Is the Dragon ... powerful by reason of
its poison? This has been a question
among scholars, and a negative
answer has been given by many. Pliny
has denied (though wrongly) all
poisonous qualities to the Dragon,
saying "The Dragon has no poison."
But seeing that it is a Serpent, and that
experience gives evidence of a contrary nature, we can put no trust in
Pliny on this point, for the Dragon
does poison the air. Some have attributed breasts to the Dragon from an
erroneous interpretation of Threnius,
Chapter IV, verse 3. It is not the
Dragon, but an animal of higher rank,
that is here meant, as Franzius clearly
shows. The evidence of our own eyes
also clearly shows it.

George Caspard Kirchmayer

A close contemporary of Conrad Gesner was the Italian Ulisse Aldrovandus, born in 1522. Aldrovandus studied medicine, graduating from the University of Bologna at the age of thirty-one, and soon became a professor there. The
success of Gesner's work may have spurred Aldrovandus to attempt a similar
project, a catalogue of everything significant in the natural world. Only three
volumes on birds appeared before his death in 1605. Between then and 1668
the remainder of his work was issued at irregular intervals. Among these
posthumous publications is Volume x: *Serpentum et Draconum Historiae
Libri Duo,* or an account of serpents and dragons in two volumes.

Aldrovandus is even more comprehensive than Gesner. Virtually all the
familiar stories of dragon lore are there. It is essentially the mixture as
before, systematically arranged, but more exhaustive in its efforts to encom-
pass everything that had ever been said on the subject of dragons. Some
interesting additions are made, however. The places where dragons are
reported include not only the areas mentioned by classical scholars but the
Alps, Atlantis, and Brazil. Atlantis is, of course, almost as problematic as
dragons themselves. The Alps, adjoining traditional dragon territory,
haunted by storms and riddled with caves, offer no surprise. But the in-
clusion of Brazil is significant.

The fifteenth and sixteenth centuries were an age of exploration and the
extent of the known world was continually being increased. Only a few
decades after Columbus had first set foot on the New World, those who had

Although certain Church authorities were beginning to doubt the efficacy of dragons as an inducement to faith, popular belief in their satanic nature remained strong. The demon Astaroth, grand treasurer of Hell (RIGHT), invariably traveled on an infernal dragon. As did the demon Asmodeus (LEFT) who was said to be the serpent who originally seduced Eve.

Dragons, once thought to roam exclusively in the remoter regions of Greece and Ethiopia, began to appear in well populated parts of France and Italy and Switzerland.

followed his footsteps were reporting that dragons existed there, just as they did in the Near and Far East. South American dragons, as they were described by European explorers, obviously had some affinity to the anacondas and other large reptiles of the Amazon basin, in the same way that the dragons of India were related to the indigenous python. Nevertheless, New World dragons were legitimate monsters, not just large snakes; they ate whole deer, men if they could get them, and were equipped with wings and other characteristics common to dragons the world over.

RIGHT AND OPPOSITE *While damsels were still subject to distress and danger from dragons and always in need of rescue by gallant knights, dragons became something of a fashionable diversion for the bored and wealthy. Catherine de Medici somehow acquired an aquatic monster to entertain guests at a water festival.*

New World dragons did not confine themselves to the hinterland of Brazil. Judging by contemporary maps, they seem to have shared the love of travel that is typical of human Americans today: their presence is depicted as far south as Patagonia and as far north as the Bering Straits. The dragon shown in Alaska may have been attracted to that inclement northern latitude by the presence, on the same map, of some elephants. Dragons, as we know, could rarely resist a challenge. Other mapmakers of the period depicted giraffes, rhinoceroses, and camels roaming over what is now Canada. Yet given that man had not yet instituted zoological gardens and parks for them

Reports of unusual dragons from abroad, such as two- and three-headed dragons in Asia (ABOVE), increased public fascination with them. The indiscriminate killing of dragons (OPPOSITE) fell into some disfavor.

Yet More Wonders of Africa

In the caues of Atlas are founde many huge and monstrous dragons, which are heauie, and of a slowe motion, bicause of their body is grosse, but their necks and tailes are slender. They are most venemous creatures, insomuch that whosoeuer is bitten or touched by them, his flesh presently waxeth soft and weake, neither can he by any means escape death.

Leo Africanus (al-Hasan ibn-Mohammed al-Wezaz al Fazi)

to inhabit, their vagrancy at the time seems credible enough. A map of northern Scandinavia, printed in 1572, also shows a dragon somewhere to the north of Lapland; it accords with the desolation of the region that it has been reduced to eating mice.

It would be a mistake to consider dragons exclusively tropical or temperate animals. It would seem to be logical that northern dragons, persecuted by Sigurd and his kind, should retreat to the empty security of the north rather than head south to a region populated by highly-experienced dragon-slayers. Indeed St. Brendan of Ireland, who long anticipated Columbus in the possibility of transatlantic travel, reported not only Leviathan in the northern seas but the active presence of dragons along the southern coast of Iceland. Since volcanoes by tradition indicate the presence of dragons, we must assume that dragons still find Iceland a congenial and stimulating refuge.

As might be expected, the deeper exploration of Africa also produced numerous accounts of "many and monstrous dragons" there. Among the travelers in Africa who described both dragons and the Hydra was the Arab diplomat, al-Hasan ibn-Mohammed, who traveled widely in the interior before he was captured and taken to Italy by pirates. Subsequently he was adopted as protégé by Pope Leo X, and is better known by his baptismal name of Leo Africanus. Leo's account of Africa was very popular in the Renaissance, and was described as "the verie best, the most particular, and methodicall that ever was written" about that continent.

An interesting European account of a journey to West Africa is included in Richard Hakluyt's *The Principall Navigations, Voiages and Discoveries of the English Nation*, printed in 1589. The voyage described is based apparently on a Robert Gainsh's first-hand experiences and observations: discussing the elephants of the region, Gainsh says that they "... have continuall warre against Dragons." But it is probable that this is influenced less by actual observation of the conflict than by familiarity with earlier accounts. On the other hand, the Venetian merchant Alvise da Ca'da Mosto, who visited Africa with a Portuguese trading expedition, was surprised to note that the serpents of Africa did not, in fact, have wings and feet "which serpents are said to possess." Such quibbling is unusual; clearly most travelers were quite content to have their expectations fulfilled. And surely the object of exploration is to broaden the imagination and fill it with enthralling and wonderful information rather than to narrow it with objective scientific curiosity.

Even if they lacked accuracy and objectivity, eyewitness accounts were

177

While the Jesuit scholar, Fr. Kircher of Switzerland, claimed no heroic personal encounters with dragons, the artist illustrating his treatise obviously felt that scientific observation alone would not hold readers' attention.

increasingly valued at the time. Aldrovandus, the professor of Bologna, provides an entertaining story with which he himself was involved. In the year 1572 a peasant was driving his ox-cart along a road near Bologna when he ran over and killed a small dragon. On examination, it proved to be a disappointing two cubits in length, roughly three feet, but despite its size it aroused considerable interest in the scientific community. The interest centered on the fact that it had only two feet, similar to those of a lizard but with four toes. And it was generally accepted by then that dragons have four feet, not two.

As Professor of Medicine, Aldrovandus was inevitably involved in the discussions of this oddity. Where had it come from? Since it lacked wings, it could scarcely be a migratory dragon from Tartary or some other distant land. Since it had four and not five toes, it could not be an Imperial dragon. Perhaps it was aquatic and had emerged from the Adriatic Sea? Or perhaps it had fallen from the heavens during a rainstorm? It could, of course, have been generated by the unnatural mating of two different species. When these and other important considerations had been earnestly debated, the conclusion was reached that the dragon was indeed some form of mutant. Eventually, when a careful drawing had been made of the remains, they were consigned to the local museum for permanent preservation and display. The peasant, incidentally, was considered to have been very fortunate in that his cart was made of ash-wood, a substance notably effective against all manner of serpents.

Another academic pursuer of dragons was the Jesuit scholar, Father Athanasius Kircher, whose *Mundus Subterraneus*, or Underground World, appeared in 1665. It is a remarkable exposition of geological theories and underground phenomena; and naturally it does not omit a section on subterranean dragons. Skeptics might be tempted to smile wryly at Kircher's prefatory remarks in this section: "There is great controversy among authors about winged dragons, whether truly in the nature of things animals of this sort exist ..." But the scholar leaves no doubt about where he himself stands on that score. He proceeds to amass irrefutable evidence that dragons, including winged ones, do exist. First of all he assembles established precedents and cites a number of familiar stories. Aldrovandus' wingless dragon is briefly referred to, with illustration; the date of the precise incident is given, but with few other details. Kircher does contribute more generously to our knowledge of dragons, however, with accounts of a number of subterranean dragons found, not in exotic and distant lands but in Switzerland, and based more or less on his own personal experience. One is described in a letter by a certain Christopher

Lions were as esoteric as dragons to Europeans, and both were notorious for their ferocity, so enmity between them was entirely plausible.

·3·A·

OPPOSITE *Artists did not readily abandon so dramatic a subject as dragon-slaying, but in Ingres' famous picture attention is focused on the beauty of the victim rather than the menace of the monster.*

A Swiss barrel-maker hibernates with dragons and lives to tell the tale.

Popular acceptance of dragons is reflected in this German drawing which, long before its time, suggests the innocuous coyness of a contemporary greeting card.

Schorer, the Prefect of Solothurn, and so every bit as reliable a witness as Fr. Kircher himself. Schorer, while admiring the serenity of the heavens one night in 1619, was surprised to see a winged dragon emerge from a cavern in the region of Mount Pilatus, near Lucerne, and fly to and fro. While it flew it emitted sparks, leading Schorer to assume at first that it was a meteor, but he soon perceived that it was a true flying dragon. It was of immense size with a long neck and tail, a serpent-like head, and ferocious gaping jaws.

Lest this should seem merely an isolated incident, Schorer supports it with two earlier compatible occurrences. In one, the skeleton of a dragon was found in his neighborhood in 1602; in the other, a dragon was encountered by a Paul Schumperlin on July 25, 1654. Schumperlin, out hunting on the slopes of the Fluhberg, came unexpectedly face to face with a dragon. Although the beast soon recoiled into its lair with a great rustling of scales, the hunter had sufficient time to examine it closely and to memorize details that tally quite closely with those of the dragon seen by Schorer himself. It too had a long neck and tail, and a head "not at all unlike" that of a horse, partly gray in color, partly flecked with white and yellow.

The countryside around Lucerne, and around Mount Pilatus in particular, seems to have been heavily infested with dragons. Another incident described by Kircher also occurred there. A native of Lucerne, a barrel-maker by trade, was wandering on the slopes of the mountain when he fell into a deep cavern. While searching vainly for a way out, he came across a pair of dragons who, unlike most of their kind, were not in the least ferocious. Possibly they were in a state of partial hibernation. The barrel-maker remained in the cave with the dragons not just for a day or two, but — according to Kircher — "for six whole months, from the 6th of November until the 10th of April" the following year. During this time, he avoided starvation by following the dragons' example and licking the moisture exuded by the walls of the cave. When spring arrived, the dragons became restive and started to stretch their wings. The man realized that they represented his only means of escape. Accordingly, he attached

181

What greater ignominy could a fearful dragon suffer than to be curbed within a bookplate?

himself to the tail of one of them and, when the dragons eventually flew out, he was carried out with them. Once outside, he dropped to the ground and so made his way home.

Like so many eyewitnesses, the hapless barrel-maker died shortly after telling his tale. It is said that the shock of returning to a normal diet was too great for his stomach. It is possible, too, that he just lost heart in the face of the inevitable skeptics. However, a monument to his remarkable escape was erected in the church of St. Leodegaris at Lucerne as permanent reproof for such doubters.

Kircher actually provides an illustration of the "two-footed and winged Swiss Dragon" in his book. This bears a striking resemblance to an "Ethiopian Dragon" shown by Aldrovandus. That in turn is almost identical to a monster shown with an account of travels in Egypt by Pierre Belon in 1554. While

The Dragon of Wantley

It is not strength that always wins,
For wit doth strength excell;
Which made our cunning champion
Creep down into a well;

Where he did think, this dragon would
    drink,
And so he did in truth;
And as he stoop'd low, he rose up and
    cry'd, "boh!"
And hit him in the mouth.

"Oh," quoth the dragon, "pox take
    thee, come out,
Thou disturb'st me in my drink:"
And then he turn'd, and s... at him;
Good lack how he did stink!

"Beshrew thy soul, thy body's foul,
Thy dung smells not like balsam;
Thou son of a whore, thou stink'st so
    sore,
Sure thy diet is unwholsome."

Our politick knight, on the other side,
Crept out upon the brink,
And gave the dragon such a douse,
He knew not what to think:

"By cock," quoth he, "say you so: do
    you see?"
And then at him he let fly
With hand and with foot, and so they
    went to 't;
And the word it was, "Hey boys,
    hey!"

Belon admits that he himself saw only preserved specimens, he describes the "winged snakes with feet" that commonly flew out of Arabia into Egypt. It will be recalled that in the fifth century B.C. Herodotus reported a similar traffic of such monsters. It could be duly argued that this similarity means that scholars have been borrowing purely imaginary drawings or descriptions of dragons from their predecessors through the centuries. But when ancient pictures or descriptions of horses resemble those we accept today, we do not use that fact to deny the existence of horses. It seems reasonable to accept that, like horses, the ordinary run of dragons have not changed much in appearance in the course of human history.

Early in the eighteenth century the credibility of dragons suffered a severe setback when the famous Swedish naturalist, Linnaeus, declared the seven-headed Hydra he was shown in Hamburg to be fabricated from animal remains.

Switzerland was not the only resort favored by dragons in the seventeenth century. A dragon that appeared to be about to sprout wings was seen in 1614 near Horsham in Sussex. Despite the fact that the author of the description did not feel safe in approaching closer than "a reasonable ocular distance," his account is quite detailed, and the names and whereabouts of other eyewitnesses are provided. It is not suggested that any of the witnesses died prematurely as a result of the experience. Another dragon appeared near Rome in either October or November of 1660. It was wounded by a hunter who, with a fine sense of tradition (and perhaps deservedly), did expire shortly afterwards, "and his whole body became of a green hue." The dragon also putrefied, unfortunately before its entire remains could be subjected to expert scrutiny. But the head and feet survived long enough to be diligently inspected by Kircher, who pronounced them genuine. Some quibbles were raised over the fact that the feet were webbed, resembling those of a goose, a characteristic not common in dragons. But there is no reason why Nature, having equipped several other related species amphibiously, should deny some dragons the same facility.

Of course there had always been a few cynics who could not fully accept the existence of dragons and other such beasts. One of these was a certain Cardanus, who scoffed when he "saw at Paris five two-footed creatures with very small wings, which one could scarcely deem capable of flight, with a small head like a Serpent, of bright color without any feathers or hair. The size of the largest of the five was about that of a small rabbit." A later commentator righteously pointed out that, "we must not, from weakness and small size of these little Dragons, rush precipitately to a conclusion regarding the whole species."

Gradually the weight of opinion veered towards disbelief, although few at the time would have gone as far as Dr. Panthot, who in 1692 unequivocally asserted all dragons to be either mythical or supernatural. Certainly, sightings became increasingly rare from the seventeenth century onwards in Europe; indeed, judging by published references, dragons became virtually invisible. The academic approach initiated by Gesner and Aldrovandus was to prove the nemesis of those dragons to whom both scholars had devoted much attention. The object of systematically describing and classifying the diverse creatures of the living world was to arrive at a clear and precise picture of that world. Certain creatures had features and properties in common that other creatures lacked. Only birds, for example, had feathers and only birds, along with insects, bats, and flying fish, could fly. Dragons, having traditionally been composed of features from every species of the animal world, simply could not be fitted into this systematic picture of creation. When scholars rejected dragons from the system, they stopped seeing dragons and discounted any evidence that they had existed.

Despite this academic rejection and a growing skepticism, the old beliefs hung on. As late as 1734, a specimen of what was claimed to be a seven-headed

While the Church may have turned its back on dragons, dragons such as this one on the altarpiece of a Spanish church continued to haunt ordinary worshipers.

As the Renaissance was replaced by the Age of Reason dragons largely retreated from public scrutiny. Their artistic existence continued, if less extravagantly. Increasingly they were reduced to the role of underlining the problems of man in pursuing a high moral purpose.

By the end of the nineteenth century the dragon had been reduced to the status of a somewhat untidy domestic pet.

Hydra could still be viewed in the city of Hamburg. Originally it had belonged to Count Königsmark, and after his death it came into the possession of the Count von Leeuwenhaupt, who offered it for sale at the staggering price of 10,000 florins. A firm of Hamburg merchants, Dreyem and Hambel, acquired it, presumably as an investment, and it was with pride that they showed it to the great Swedish naturalist, Carl von Linné, known as Linnaeus, when he visited Hamburg. Linnaeus was considerably impressed and commented on the notable skill of the craftsmen who had concocted from the parts of a variety of animals so convincing a fake. Messrs. Dreyem and Hambel were, naturally, outraged. Linnaeus was threatened with prosecution for defaming their property, and left Hamburg hurriedly. The new zoology had lost a first skirmish with the old, but has won every other skirmish since. It would be premature, however, to say which will win the war, particularly since the old zoology has on its side such ferocious allies.

Beginning in the nineteenth century, there dawned an era that was to worship rationalism and the scientific method above all else. While dragons seemed to have retreated from the civilized world, their presence over thousands of years of human history and their effect on men's actions and thoughts had to be rationalized. Unless their ghosts were exorcised by commonsense explanation, they would continue to haunt mankind.

Initially it was thought probable that there had once been monstrous serpents larger than those that had survived into the modern world, and that primitive man, unenlightened by education and Christian values, had allowed his fears to magnify the creatures further and to add to them the awesome powers and attributes that dragons were supposed to possess. To the Christian rationalist, ignorance, pagan superstition, and doubts about the benefits of reason and progress were evils as challenging as dragons, and he, like St. George, had to confront and slay them.

Darwin's theories focus public scrutiny on the origin of flying monsters.

Darwin's theories of evolution intensified the Victorian interest in the long story of the past. They may have incensed fundamental Christians who believed that the past had been adequately chronicled in Holy Writ, but they did provide also some evidence that the world had once been populated by monsters as vast and as ferocious as dragons, some of which had even had the ability to fly. The study of fossilized bones of extinct animals became the fashionable science amongst both amateurs and professionals, and was a favorite topic in drawing and dining rooms. Mrs. Jameson, author of a two-volume work on *Sacred and Legendary Art*, related that "Professor Owen told me that the head of a dragon in one of the legendary pictures ... in Italy ... closely resembled in form that of the *Deinotherium Giganteum*." Since Deinotherium happens to be a relative of the modern elephant, this might seem an inappropriate basis for the dragon also; but then, as we know from human experience, family feuds have always been the most intense. "At Aix," Mrs. Jameson related further, "a huge fossilized head of one of the Sauri was for a long time preserved as head of the identical dragon subdued by St. Martha; and St. Jerome relates that he himself beheld in Tyre the bones of

PREVIOUS PAGE *It is only recently that man has matched dragon in the destructive use of concentrated energy.*

the sea monster to which Andromeda had been exposed." The exhibited head of another dragon proved to be that of a woolly rhinoceros.

Such scientific disenchantments were partially countered by the efforts of a number of popular Victorian novelists, among them Arthur Conan Doyle (who confined pure reason to his Sherlock Holmes series): one of their most successful themes of fantasy involved the discovery of some unexplored cavern or valley still inhabited by one or many prehistoric monsters. This increased the popularity of the theory that dragons may have been surviving members of extinct species; it also provided an ambiguous reassurance to those Christians who had the Bible's word for it that dragons had existed. It is significant that in more than a century, despite all scientific evidence discounting the possibility of surviving or reborn monsters, the popular

Sulking dragons would have turned over in their caves had they been aware of the contempt imposed on them in this Victorian tableau.

NIGHT'S SWIFT DRAGONS CUT THE CLOUDS FULL FAST

appetite for books or films about such threatening apparitions has created a major entertainment industry.

In China, where dragons maintained a tenuous existence, the interest in fossil bones was commercial rather than intellectual. Well into the twentieth century, rich fossil deposits were being mined and marketed widely as parts of dragons; as one paleontologist put it, "dragon's teeth and dragon's bones can be obtained from every better-class apothecary's shop, providing one has the necessary prescription and sufficient money; for everything originating from such a huge beast must be a powerful therapeutic agent, and for this reason alone is expensive." So widespread was this fraudulent trade in fossil bones that European paleontologists, in search of specimens for their studies, found it more fruitful to go to apothecaries' stores in Chinese towns than to the fossil beds.

In nineteenth century Europe then, the prehistoric dinosaur and his kin seemed ideally suited to play the role of dragon. Specifically, the flying pterodactyl, which was reptilian, could fly and was said to have enormous jaws, looked the part. Even if such a monster could not have survived into those eras when dragons were said to exist, wasn't it possible that some sort of folk memory had projected those prehistoric images into ancient, classical, and medieval imaginations? Even today those who feel that there must be some rational explanation for the tenacity of belief in dragons cling to the

In England dragons were driven to posing for illustrations in children's books of fairy tales.

In Germany dragons were recruited to help bolster an increasingly flamboyant sense of Teutonic self-esteem. Once again they had to endure Siegfried's brutality.

idea that it is rooted in some vestigial recollection of pterodactyls or the like. As surviving Victorian exhibits in museums show, the inspiration for reconstruction of prehistoric animals seemed often to be dragons rather than dinosaurs; some reconstructions show more than a dim recollection of dragonesque features and seem incomplete without a mannequin dressed up in St. George's shining armor.

There is, unfortunately, one crucial piece of evidence that utterly demolishes the attractive and plausible theory of prehistoric recollection. The

facts are that dinosaurs, along with pterodactyls, became extinct about seventy million years ago, and that man's remote ancestors evolved only three or four million years ago, sixty-seven million years too late to catch a glimpse of the massive brutes. Elephants, too, were about as many years too late to confront pterodactyls. Carl G. Jung, the eminent psychologist, advanced the theory that we all share a collective unconscious in which is submerged all the images of what has happened to the race of man. It would be stretching that theory to suggest that the small, primitive, and obscure mammals that shared the world with the dinosaurs and that eventually evolved into man could have deposited the vast images of monsters in that memory.

And so, while it is still possible to speculate that early encounters with massive fossil bones, like early encounters and stories about pythons and crocodiles, may have stimulated man's conception of dragons, we must admit that dragons are not directly related to any ordinary creature we know of. Is it then purely a creature of the imagination? It would be unfair to pass over the theory of Carl Jung without touching on another important aspect of it: he did not suggest that the collective unconscious was filled with merely pictorial images of man's history, that might emerge into the subconscious in dreams and at times of psychosis, but with what he called archetypes — symbolic representations of concepts that are common to all men at all times in all cultures, such as the wise old man, the mother, the young hero ... and possibly, the dragon-monster? But exploring that possibility, perhaps we had better account for the unhappy lot of dragons in our own era.

It should be acknowledged first of all that, for all its obvious bad points, the dragon has shown an unparalleled will to survive. Would man himself have survived the enmity of centuries of gods and heroes, much less persistent doubt of his existence? On the other hand, the dragon has always commanded a widespread support and credibility amongst simple ordinary people, one that any politician might envy and that persists to this day.

Given the choice, dragons would probably prefer the unflattering return fight with St. George by Dürer (ABOVE) to a decadent relationship with an effete King Arthur as composed by Aubrey Beardsley (OPPOSITE).

A Red Dragon

A scaled and horned dragon, believed by many to be a supernatural creature, has made its appearance in Kiangsi, the communist-ridden province, according to a letter from Mr. Huang Wen-chih, formerly President of the Hankow General Chamber of Commerce.

Mr. Huang writes from Nanchang saying that the dragon was seen on the Han River, the principal river in Kiangsi, about half a month ago. He adds that the presence of the dragon is the cause of the flood between Nanchang and Feng-cheng, which are some 200 *li* apart. Most of the houses in that region have been inundated during the past two weeks.

As the Book of History recorded that some two thousand years ago the people used to offer the fairest maiden every year to the Ho Po, or the God of the River, to be his concubine, it is now suggested that some suitable sacrifice should be presented to the dragon. It is said that if his wrath is appeased, the flood will subside. On the other hand, if nothing is done to please the creature, it would make the Kiangsi people suffer more besides the flood and the communist uprisings.

East or west, the domestic disputes of dragons have always caused violent climatic disturbances.

A scaly, horned dragon causes floods and civil unrest.

Belief in dragons at its simplest is exemplified by the common faith in the efficacy of dragon's blood. In the late nineteenth century, it was normal for a girl forsaken by her lover to buy "two pennyworth of dragon's blood." This she would throw on the fire while uttering the following:

*'Tis not this blood I wish to burn
But ....'s heart I wish to turn.
May he neither sleep or rest
Till he has granted my request.*

So ingrained was this belief that in 1920 a writer felt it necessary to discount as a fallacy "that the substance called Dragon's Blood is the dried blood of a dragon." In the interim the substance had continued in much demand as a love potion, with a great resurgence during World War 1, following a brief decline.

As has been mentioned, reports of dragons continue in the Far East. Roads in Hong Kong have been reported washed away because the surveyors had neglected the obvious precaution of investigating the attitudes of the tutelary dragons in the district. In 1931 a "scaled and horned dragon" was seen in the Kiangsi province of China. Its presence was attested by no less person than a former President of the Hankow General Chamber of Commerce and it was blamed for floods and civil insurrection in the area. More recently a dragon lived in the waters of the Mekong River in front of the Lan Xang hotel in the Laotian capital Vientiane, sharing those waters with the giant catfish for which they are famous. During the summer of 1966 it emerged from its lair and played a devious role in the politics of the neutralist coalition government of the day.

In the west, recently reported dragons have been mainly aquatic. In northern Europe, not unexpectedly, the survivors show a family likeness to the ancestral Serpent of Midgard. As northern forests were cleared and the land came to be fully exploited, these fabulous beasts were obliged to evade excessive scrutiny by taking refuge in the deep and mysterious lakes and fjords that abound in the region. The Loch Ness Monster is, of course, the most celebrated of these aquatic monsters. Its ancestry is impeccable. The first recorded sighting was about A.D. 565, when St. Columba banished it from his presence. This sets it firmly in the tradition of dragons slain or subdued by saints, a sort of negative martyrdom. Since that date, more and more people have claimed to have seen the Monster, not in the least abashed by continued failure to find tangible remains or irrefutable evidence that it actually exists but continually encouraged by an archive of photographs that purport to show the creature

Despite a new realism in art, the most endearing elements of mythology and folklore were captured in the whimsical fantasies of the Grimm brothers.

cavorting in the loch. To prove conclusively that it does not exist is an impossibility. Mere unlikelihood is not enough. In this respect too, the Loch Ness Monster may be very much part of the wider dragon tradition, but it is unique in being the first modern dragon to have attracted and yet evaded a vast panoply of research teams over the years, equipped variously with batteries of cameras, flotillas of boats and submersible vehicles, and even with underwater television equipment. Possibly its problem is just shyness.

As Scots from other areas are quick to point out, Loch Ness holds no monopoly on monsters. If all the legends of monsters were to be credited, there is scarcely a loch in Scotland that lacks a monster. Lochs Lochy, Oich, Quoich, Arkaig, Fine, and the Gareloch all have their stories of strange and fearsome beasts, whether straightforward monsters, or the distinctively Gaelic *each uisge,* or "water horse." What these and lesser lochs seem to share is the lack of an experienced and enterprising local tourist board.

The same is true of Ireland, homeland of the dragon-slaying Finn. Without a dragon or water-monster ever having been captured, stories persist from the earliest days to the present, a fact that confirms either the legendary richness of Irish imagination or the elusiveness of Irish dragons. The Irish are

Elusive Scottish water-monsters evade prying eyes.

RIGHT AND OPPOSITE *As creatures of tradition, dragons probably yearn for the swashbuckling days of St. George whenever they are confronted by modern images of themselves.*

Rejected by an inimical and pragmatic world, dragons over the past century have retreated to remote sanctuaries. Lake Erie is said to be one such refuge and may have inspired this Pennsylvania-Dutch folk art.

Dragons sighted from the Bering Straits to Tierra del Fuego.

not dogmatic on the question of dragons: a monster has been observed in Lough Ree several times in the past few decades, but it is conceded that it might instead have been a family of otters, a coelacanth, a midget Russian submarine dropped from the air, or maybe just "Councillor D'Arcy out for a swim."

Scandinavia, the true birthplace of the prolific Serpent of Midgard, should not be neglected. The Skrimsl of Iceland was sighted as recently as 1860, and a monster in Sweden's Lake Storsjö appeared many times up to 1907 and then, after a prolonged absence, just following the end of World War II.

Europe is no more the exclusive domain of dragons now than it ever was. Many North American Indian tribes have a legendary history of similar monsters, backed up in recent times by eyewitness reports. Lakes Erie, Ontario, Utah, and many others claimed the presence of dragons during the nineteenth century, with sporadic sightings persisting into the 1960s. In South America, a lake in Patagonia was menaced by a monster. And in Africa, dragonesque monsters have been reported from numerous areas, particularly in the Congo, Nile, and Zambesi basins. Even New Zealand can call a dragon its own "in size a monstrous whale, in shape like a hideous dragon."

These monsters, for all their diversity and dispersal, have much in common. They tend to live in very deep or very remote lakes and swamps; the frequency with which they are reported diminishes in proportion to the accessibility of their haunts. Modern sightings occur most often in locations with strong folk traditions of monsters, a fact that, depending on one's prejudices, either enhances or detracts from the credibility of the eyewitnesses. Finally — and this seems a definitive feature of modern monsters — they are quite exceptionally elusive.

Such observations, interpreted by a skeptical mind, might seem to support the conclusion that if dragons existed at all they existed only as figments of imagination. But set against what is known about dragons and their character-

The Haida Indians of the American northwest provide this rather touching glimpse of the dragon as a lonely recluse.

istics, their present-day elusiveness may be interpreted as support for quite the opposite conclusion.

Dragons have always been elusive. At certain periods in their history, when subjected to provocation and persecution by gods and heroes, they have seemed more evident and more destructive than at others. In the past certain dragons, because of an inordinate greed for sheep or virgins or elephants or ordinary citizens, have attracted notoriety and savage reprisal. But obviously all that is past history.

Like ourselves, dragons realize that they are living in a radically changed world. Even though there may be no gods and few heroes left with whom they have to deal, dragons appreciate that today's society would not tolerate – and has massive means to punish – the kind of behavior a few misguided dragons were guilty of in the past. As study of the history of dragons during the Middle

Ages and the Renaissance will confirm, the species has been conscientious in adjusting itself to changing times. Unfortunately, mankind's response has been far from conscientious and less than generous.

Despite all the slings and arrows and lances they may have had to endure in more violent times, dragons obviously find the skepticism and ridicule to which they are subjected today even harder to bear. And so, no longer inclined to react with destructive anger, they have for the most part acted as any human would act in similar circumstances – they have secluded themselves from an inimical world. That is why in our time dragons are so rarely seen, and why, when they are reported, it is from regions where the dragon's place in the order of things has been traditionally acknowledged. It is significant, for instance, that in China, where dragons have always been accorded respect and generosity and have always responded in kind, dragons are seen more often than elsewhere.

It should not be assumed, however, that all dragons have meekly accepted their present unhappy lot. It should be recalled that from earliest times dragons have been associated with the weather, and also with earthquakes and

RIGHT AND OPPOSITE *On the whole, northern dragons seem to have fared better than those elsewhere. But it seems obvious that today's gods and heroes are unworthy of their mettle. They can only relive in memory the excitement of the great days of the Nordic past.*

volcanoes. Surely it underlines the naiveté of modern man that, despite all our scientific gadgetry and computerization, we have yet to succeed in accurately predicting the weather, much less controlling it. Despite all their disastrous failures, resulting in inexplicable storms and floods and periods of drought, meteorologists will never admit that dragons deserve a crucial place in their calculations, neither will they put aside their charts and print-outs and attempt instead to propitiate the few disgruntled dragons responsible for our climatic misfortunes.

In respect of earthquakes and volcanoes, scientific man's ignorance is even more – to use a *mot juste* – abysmal. Typhon is still imprisoned beneath Mount Etna and, as recent eruptions have demonstrated, is as violently resentful as he was when he was cast down there by Zeus. Apart from that and

Rarely do dragons indulge in the kind of mischievous pranks that make magpies lovable villains.

many other long-imprisoned volcanic dragons, there is recent evidence that another dragon has had to be incarcerated off the coast of Iceland, a country with a long history of dragons. While earthquakes occur regularly in the areas traditionally inhabited by dragons, such as China, the Near East, and South America, it is noteworthy also that a dragon beneath the state of California had been increasingly restive over the past century. It is symptomatic of the times that despite California's reputation as a breeding ground of ostentatious crusading politicians, no hero has yet been found who will dare the dragon to emerge from the Andreas Fault and do battle.

Even if we reject such evidence and persist in believing that dragons have never been more than creatures of fantasy and legend, we are confronted by their *persistence* in the human imagination. If he had given more extensive thought to the subject, the late Carl Jung would probably have concluded that the dragon is an archetype, a symbolic creature necessary to stimulate heroism in each of us. But we do not need to study psychology, nor delve into the collective unconscious to arrive at the conclusion that we probably need dragons more than they need us. We have only to recollect what stories we prefer to read and what films we prefer to watch to realize that if dragons did not exist it would be necessary to invent them.

Isn't it strikingly significant that since dragons have begun to seclude themselves from us, our need for invented monsters and threatening creatures of every kind has increased? To take one of the more recent examples,

During the Napoleonic wars armies adopted the dragon to emphasize the destructive power of their cannons.

the movie *Jaws*, about an aquatic monster that menaced a community and was ultimately worsted in combat by a pair of contemporary heroes, was one of the most popular movies of all time. The equally popular science fiction novel, *The Kraken Wakes*, dealt with the return of a traditional aquatic monster, attended by floods and disaster. And the popular Japanese film, *Rodan*, continues to confront late night television viewers with a dragonesque flying monster.

As will have been obvious in this history, the dragon is protean; it can appear in many guises, frequently symbolizing the pressing concerns and the traditional beliefs of those who observe it. Since modern man sustains

Whether dragons today assume a traditional or a mystical aspect, evidence of their continued presence still haunts the corners of men's minds in the eternal struggle of good over evil.

the dubious credo that he knows all there is to know about himself and his world, the dragon must assume myriad ambiguous forms as a menacing extraterrestrial presence in numerous other science fiction novels and films. The purveyors of such entertainments invariably claim that they are only giving the public what it wants. While their assertions may be self-serving, they are not necessarily untrue. The elusive dragon, however, does not confine itself to fiction or entertainment: political and social cartoonists have commonly used the image of a serpentine monster with gaping jaws to symbolize the vast threatening evils of corruption, crime, inflation, and bureaucracy to the individual citizen. When we consider the effectiveness of such uses and such adaptations, we may be prompted to reflect in gratitude that nothing became the dragon in this world like his leaving it.

But in reality, the long history of dragons continues. Dragons have accompanied mankind since its beginnings and, in one guise or another, will continue to do so. The history of dragons is the stuff that man is made of; the study of dragons is the study of the human mind.

RIGHT *It is possible that some damsels exploited the known weakness of dragons for a pretty face.*

OPPOSITE *If we are to believe St. John and certain latter day prophets, we may witness the ultimate battle between Behemoth and Leviathan any day now.*

Acknowledgments

Archiv für Kunst und Geschichte, Berlin 13, 16, 18, 22 & 23, 25 (*above left and below*), 26, 27, 28, 31, 32, 35, 54, 55, 77, 82, 88, 90, 94, 95, 97, 101, 114, 118, 120, 122, 123, 128 (*above*), 132, 133, 137, 139, 140, 144, 145, 147 (*above*), 150, 151 (*right*), 161, 166 (*left*), 179, 182, 193, 196, 201, 203, 205. *Bettmann Archive, New York City* 46, 63, 85 (*below*). *Bildarchiv Foto Marburg* 33, 72, 78, 91, 96 (*above*), 121, 147 (*above*), 148 (*left*), 151 (*left*). *Bodleian Library, Oxford* 25, 102, 104, 105, 106, 107, 108 (*above left*), 124, 135, 165, 169 (*above left*), 173 (*below*). *British Museum, London* 29 (*below*), 117, 172, 173. *J. E. Bulloz, Paris* 77, 135, 142, 195, 206. *Cooper-Bridgeman Library,* 149. *Deutsche Fotothek, Dresden* 12, 29, 37 (*above*), 112, 143, 146, 181 (*above*). *C. M. Dixon, Dover* 100. *Escher Foundation, Haags Gemeentemuseum, The Hague* 199. *Mary Evans Picture Library, London* 34, 38, 140, 157, 165, 171, 177, 178, 183. *Werner Forman Archive, London* 20, 24, 42, 47, 49, 52, 53, 61. *Fotomas Index, London* 126, 131 (*below*), 159, 168 (*above*), 170, 202, 204 (*below*). *John R. Freeman, London* 125, 128, 129, 154. *Sonia Halliday, Turville* 39, 92, 93. *Robert Harding Associates, London* 40 (*above*), 64, 138, 152, 198, 205 (*left*). *Michael Holford, Loughton* 40 (*below*), 60, 75, 103, 156. *The Hildebrand Brothers* 188 & 189. *Angelo Hornak, London* 192. *Internationale Bilderagentur, Zurich* 110. *Lambeth Palace Library* (with kind permission of His Grace the Archbishop of Canterbury and the Trustees of the Library) 131 (*above*). *Lauros-Giraudon, Paris* 85 (*above*), 137 (*above*), 155. *Lichtbildwerkstätte Alpenland, Vienna* 153. *William MacQuitty, London* 17, 19, 21, 50, 65. *The Mansell Collection, London* 10 & 11, 14, 15, 51, 69, 70, 71, 73, 75, 80, 84, 160, 168 (*below*), 186 (*left*), 191. *Musée des Beaux Arts, Montreal* 9. *Museum of Fine Arts, Boston* 200. *National Gallery, London* 174, 180, 186 (*right*). *Bury Peerless, Birchington* 43, 44. *Photoresources, Dover* 79, 98, 99. *Picturepoint, London* 86 & 87, 113, 119, 130, 153, 158, 207. *Radio Times Hulton Picture Library, London* 81. *Scala, Florence* 30, 66 & 67, 83, 141, 162 & 163, 166 & 167, 175. *Ronald Sheridan, Harrow-on-the-Hill* 148 (*right*). *Snark International, Paris* 37, 38, 115, 127, 136, 169. *SPADEM, Paris* 93, 134. *University of London, London* 187. *University Museum of National Antiquities, Oslo* 89. *Victoria and Albert Museum, London* (Crown Copyright) 48, 56, 57, 116, 176, 185, 194. *Wallace Collection, Miniature Gallery, London* 76.

Although every effort has been made to insure that permissions for all material were obtained, those sources not formally acknowledged here will be included in all future editions of this book.

Illustrations

9 Jason charming the Dragon, Salvator Rosa, 1615-1673. **10 & 11** Bel fights Tiamat/engraving from the Nineveh marbles. **12** Babylonian enamel wall relief. **13** Assyrian world serpent. **14 & 15** Bas-relief on the walls of the palace of Assur-nasir-pal, king of Assyria, about 885-860 BC. **15** Assyrian cylinder seal. **18** Bes, Egyptian deity, sixth century BC. **19** Tomb of Seti I. **20** Killing of Apophis from The Book of the Dead, 21st dynasty. **21** Winged serpent, Cairo. **22 & 23** Die Bilder zur Bibel, Matthaus Merian, 1593-1650. **24** Aztec featherwork shield. **24** Tlazolteotl, from Codex Fejervary-Mayer. **25** Codex Laud, English, 15th century. **25 (below)** Die Bilder zur Bibel, Matthaus Merian, 1593-1650. **26 & 27** Ibid. **28** St. Wolfgang and the Devil, Michael Pacher, 1438-1498. **29 (below)** Variations in the first and second editions of Luther's translation of the New Testament, with woodcuts by Lucas Cranach. **30** Bottega di Gherardo di Giovanni, from Museo degli Innocenti, Florence. **31** Archangel as dragon-slayer, unknown master, 1500. **32** Eve and the Serpent by Gunther Zainer, 1470. **34** Dragon and Behemoth, 12th century MS. **35** Daniel's vision from the Old Testament, Matthaus Merian, 1593-1650. **36** Apocalypse, Jean Duvet, 1485-1561. **37 (above)** Apocalypse, Gerard Groenning. **37 (below)** Apocalypse de Bamberg, German, anonymous. **39** French stained glass, 14th century. **40 (below)** Rustam and horse Rakhsh kill dragon, from the Shanameh by Firdanis. **41** Persian MS. **42** Vishnu and Ananta, from the National Gallery, Prague. **47** Buddha seated on Mucilinda, 12th century. **49** Badge of mandarin, 17th century. **50** Tomb rubbing, Han dynasty. **52** Mother of pearl decorative inlay. **53** Robe with imperial dragon, 19th century. **56** Chinese watercolor. **57** Sadahide triptych. **60** Embroidered emperor's robe. **61** Painted 17th century screen. **62** Chair cover, 19th century. **64** Ming lacquer plaque. **66 & 67** Perseus frees Andromeda, Piero di Cosimo, Uffizi, Florence. **71** Chimera bronze. **76** Perseus and Andromeda, F. le Moyne, 1688-1737. **77** Etruscan vase. **77** Cadmus and the Dragon, Louvre, Paris. **82** Aktaeon and Artemis, Guiseppe Cesari. **86 & 87** St. George and the Dragon, Paolo Uccello, 1396-1475. **88** De Architektura, Marcus Polonius Vitruvius, first century BC. **89** Animal head post or prow from the Oseberg find. **90** Thor and the Serpent of Midgard, Johann Heinrich Füssli, 1741-1825. **91** Detail from medieval bestiary, Leningrad. **92** Angers tapestry, 14th century. **93** Stained glass, St. John the Baptist. **94** Liber Chronicarum, Hartmann Schedel, circa 1515. **95** Angers tapestry, 14th century. **96** Michael's struggle with the dragon, Albrecht Dürer, 1471-1528. **97** Apocalypse, Albrecht Dürer, 1471-1528. **98** Runestone depicting Harald Bluetooth, King of Denmark, AD 985. **99** Woodcarving, Sigurd kills Fafnir. **100** German 14th century altarpiece. **101** Liber Chronicarum, Hartmann Schedel. **102** MS Douce Apocalypse, Heraldry, English, pre-1272. **103** Apocalypse tapestry, Angers, 14th century. **104** MS Ashmole, English, circa 1200. **106** English MS, circa 1400. **106 (below)** 13th century MS. **111** From the Travels of Sir John Mandeville. **113** Death of Gincelin and fight between Morbidus and the sea monster. **114** Swiss griffin, 1450. **115** From the Voyages of Marco Polo. **118** Cerberus. **119** Alexander borne up by griffins. **120** Holzschnitt aus dem "Seelentrost," 14th century, unknown master. **121** Sacred and profane miniature. **122** 14th century alchemy. **123** 15th century alchemy. **126** Witchcraft. **127** M. Maier, 1618. **128 (above)** Tapestry, Historisches Museum, Basle. **128 (below)** From Arts of the Alchemists, 1652. **129** Ibid. **130** The Conjunction of Opposites. **131 (below)** Occult Philosophy, Book II. **132** "Splendor Solis," Augsburg, 17th century. **133** Uroboros, 15th century. **135** St. George, Bulgarian, 1684. **136** St. George, Roger van der Weyden, National Gallery, Washington. **137** Museum of Catalan Art, Barcelona. **137** St. George, Vittore Carpaccio, 1460-1523. **139** St. George, Lucas Cranach, 1472-1553. **140** St. George circa 1400. **141** St. George and the Dragon, Paolo Uccello, 1396-1475. **142** St. George, Raphael, Louvre, Paris. **143** St. George by an unknown master. **145** St. George, Lucas Cranach, 1472-1553. **146** St. George, 1470. **148** St. Michael, French, 15th century. **148 (left)** St. Michael, altarpiece, 1340. **149** St. Michael and the Dragon, Bartolomeo Bermejo, Barcelona, 1470. **150** St. Margaret, Michael Wolgemut, 1434-1519. **151 (left)** St. Margaret, Lucas Cranach, 1513. **151 (right)** St. Margaret, Giulio Romano, 1493-1546. **152** German embroidery depicting the story of Tristam. **153** Percival's View of the New Law and the Old. **154** From Arts of the Alchemists. **155** Tres Riches Heures du duc de Berry. **156** Harold's men are killed. From the Bayeux tapestry. **157** Device of François I. **158** Henry VI's arms. From a MS in the British Museum. **159** The arms of Oliver Cromwell. **160** The arms of Gray's Inn, London. **161** Apocalypse, Hartmann Schedel, 15th century. **162 & 163** Tapestry from Wawel Castle, Cracow. **165** Dragons, circa 1150. **166** Sea monster, 1630. **166 & 167** La Caduta degli Angelli Ribelli, P. Breughel the Elder, c 1525-1569. **168 (below)** Munster's Cosmographia Universalis, 1550. **169 (above left)** English Romanesque. **169** Dragons fashioned from rays. **172 & 173 (above)** Dictionnaire Infernal, L. Breton, Paris, 1863. **173** 13th century English MS. **174** Tintoretto, 1518-1594, National Gallery, London. **175** Tapestry of Catherine de Medici, Uffizi, Florence. **176** Albrecht Dürer 1471-1528. **177** Munster's Cosmographia Universalis, 1550. **178** Father Kircher's Mundus Subterraneus. **179** Dragon and Lion, Zoan Andrea. **180** Ingres, 1780-1867, National Gallery, London. **181 & 182** Hans Thoma, 1839-1924. **183** The Dragon of Wantley. **184** The hydra seen by Linnaeus. **185** Spanish altarpiece. **186 (left)** A Pilgrim's Progress, John Bunyan. **186 (right)** St. Michael, Carlo Crivelli. **188 & 189** Smaug. **191** Engraving, J. G. Lough. **192** Illustration to d'Aulnoy's Fairy Tales, G. R. Browne. **193** Siegfried kills the dragon, Aquarell, 1900. **194** Aubrey Beardsley's illustration to Morte d'Arthur, Alfred Tennyson. **195** St. George, Albrecht Dürer, 1471-1528. **196** Drachenkampf in der Jura-Zeit, Thomas Hawkins. **197** Illustration from the Grimm Brothers. **199** Dragon, M.C. Escher, Escher Foundation, The Hague. **200** Pennsylvania-Dutch frakturart, Museum of Fine Arts, Boston. **202** Ring of the Nibelung, Arthur Rackham. **203** Siegfried killing Fafnir. **204 (above)** Max Klinger, 1857-1920. **205** Tarot card, 19th century, British Museum. **206** Balzac illustrated by Gustave Doré, 1855 edition. **207** Leviathan and Behemoth, William Blake, 1757-1827.